MW01624619

TASTE OF BAVARIA

Typical recipes and impressions

MONIKA SCHUSTER | ANNA CAVELIUS

TASTE OF BAVARIA

Typical recipes and impressions

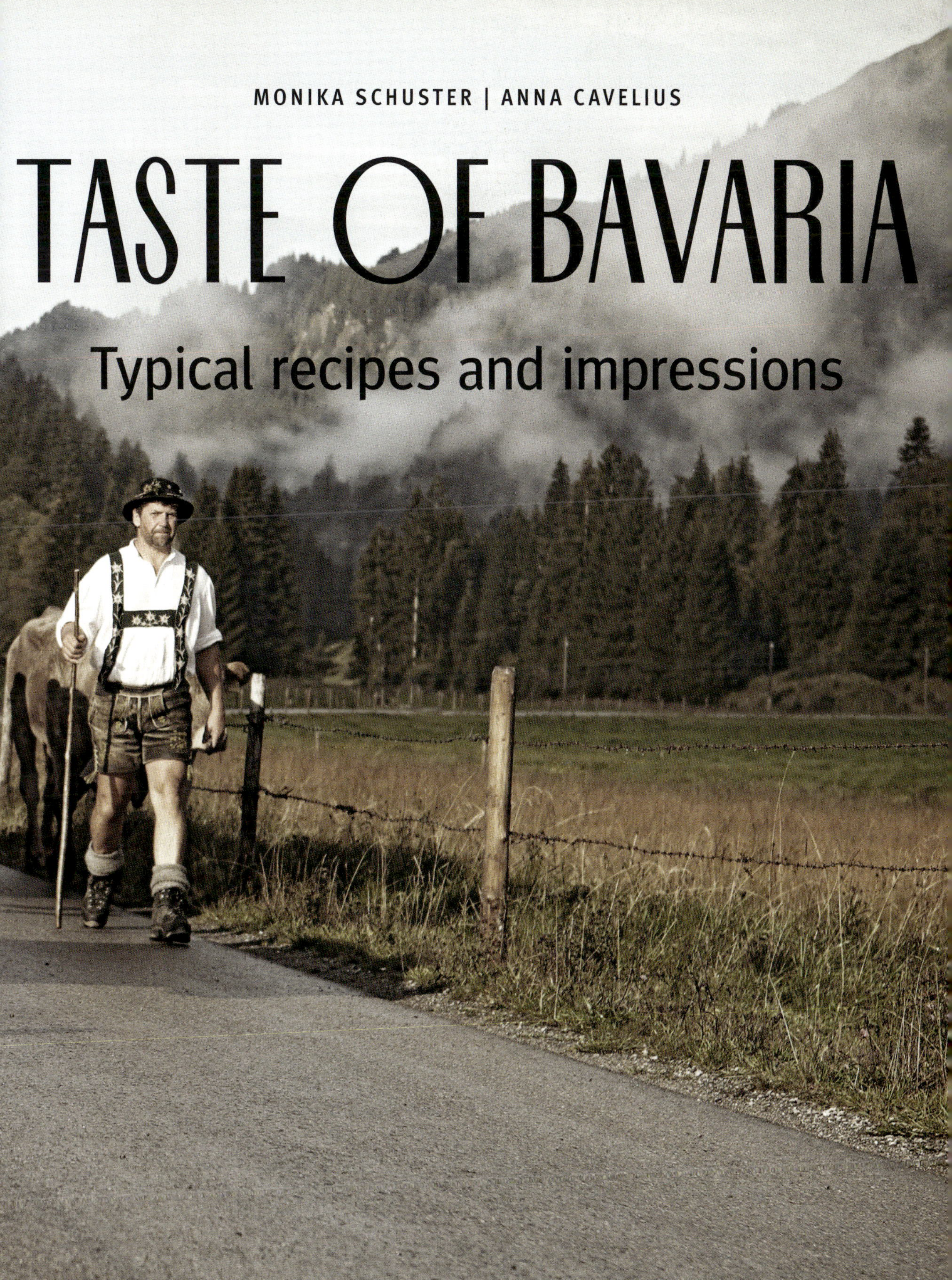

CONTENTS

FRIDAY FOOD PAGES 98-127

Bavarians are Catholic, so Fridays – their day of penance – are meat-free. But that doesn't bother them at all, because they are just as fond of fish dishes or of course their beloved yeast dumplings.

LOVELY LEFTOVERS PAGES 128-147

Bavarians don't like letting things go to waste! And so, rather than into the bin, any leftovers go into the next dish, beautifully prepared and complemented by other ingredients – cheap and cheerful.

FESTIVE FEASTS PAGES 148-213

Holidays are a special time in Bavaria. The girls and boys all dress up to look their best – and things get pretty nice and tasty in the kitchen, too.

SWEET SEVENTH HEAVEN PAGES 214-235

... is where Bavaria's top treats will take you. Whether it be a doughnut in the morning, a cream puff in the afternoon, or a raspberry cream in the evening – you've got to have something sweet.

OFF TO THE PEAKS OF PLEASURE!

Bavarian cuisine – much like the Bavarians themselves – is perhaps a little rough, a little bitter and a little heavy. But those who think it's summed up by pork knuckle and dumplings are greatly mistaken. Let's get rid of this cliché once and for all! As you make your way to the peaks of Bavarian cuisine, you'll discover all its unique, heavenly pleasures! The dishes are subtly elegant, usually simple, exquisitely honest, authentic and tasty – and always top-class.

Bavarian cooking is packed full of traditions its people are particularly proud of, and they foster and preserve them with great care. Nothing is wasted. This is perfectly exemplified by the Munich Kocherlball, or Cooks' Ball, which has become a huge annual event. People meet on a Sunday morning by the Chinese Tower in the English Garden to commemorate all the servants – from kitchenhands to cooks to stable workers – who, in the 19th century, would gather here every Sunday at the crack of dawn before getting back to their hard work. People would chat, dance, kiss and eat. They didn't have much, but they made the most of what little they had. That's the Bavarians for you: making something out of nothing!

Bavaria has virtually achieved a cult status, and not just during the Oktoberfest! The home-grown recipes from times past, and for all manner of occasions, are today more relevant than ever. And they all fit into our "neatly packed rucksack", which effortlessly transports everyone – locals, visitors and Bavaria fans alike – to the region's culinary peaks. What you do need, however, are proper regional products, like healthy cattle, who love being out in the fresh Bavarian air, and flavoursome vegetables and herbs, which thrive in our wonderful soil.

So now it's your turn to embark on your culinary ramble and scale unimaginable heights. We're sure you'll make it. And if you have the odd problem, don't give up; just keep at it. Because the only way to get better is to actually get into the kitchen and start cooking. We would certainly love for you to reach the top and proclaim that "Bavarian food is awesome and tastes simply delicious!"

Monika Schuster   Anna Cavelius

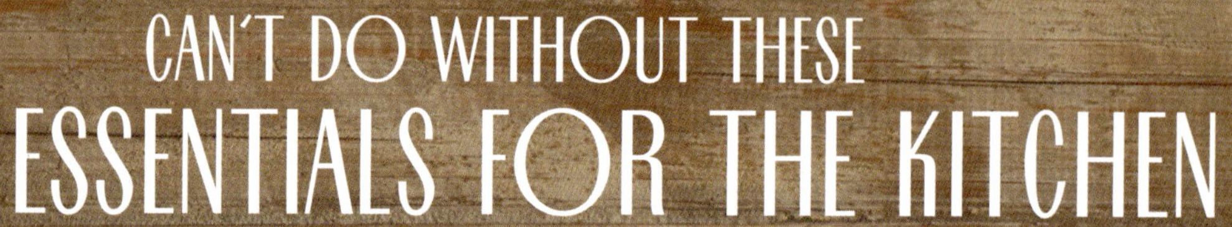

CAN'T DO WITHOUT THESE ESSENTIALS FOR THE KITCHEN

hot, wholegrain
and sweet mustard
horseradish (fresh or
from a jar)

various vegetable
oils, such as
sunflower oil,
rapeseed oil
and grape seed oil

cider vinegar
white vinegar
white wine
vinegar

dill
lovage
bay leaves (fresh
or dried)
parsley
chives

spice mixtures such as
pickled beef spices and
gingerbread spices

spiral slicer
and cutter
for radishes
sieve
box grater
potato ricer
nutmeg grater
disposable
straining cloth
(or use a
kitchen towel)
butter
clarified butter
lard
allspice
berries
caraway seeds,
whole and
ground
juniper
berries
also useful:
roasting tin
handheld blender
pestle and mortar
cloves, fennel seeds
black peppercorns
coriander seeds
nutmeg
250 GRAMM
Schweine-
Fett

BROTZEIT IS THE BEST TIME

Since there's nothing Bavarians love more than eating in the open air, we've got your Brotzeit picnic baskets covered – from sausage and radish salads to brawn. So it's off to the beer garden, where a fresh Bavarian beer awaits!

large pretzels
farmhouse bread
butter

table cloth, napkins
cutting boards and/or plates
cutlery, bread knife
salt, pepper

BROTZEIT BASKET

ALL THIS IS INSIDE

LIQUIDS DO NOT BREAK THE FAST

Such was the pious and strictly followed rule. So it's no wonder then that the art of beer brewing in the early Middle Ages was particularly cultivated at the Bavarian monasteries, where praying and working (Latin: orare and laborare), as well as the fasting times in between, were often exceptionally hard. The monks therefore applied their Christian diligence and zeal to refining their fasting beverages. The strongly brewed beer they produced was in fact greatly beneficial, and nourished the impoverished friars enough for them to continue working and praying. It also unquestionably brightened their mood. Each of the brothers would ultimately receive five helpings (or measures) a day. And the quantity which later became the Mass (meaning measure) was the equivalent of one to two litres of the delicious brew. So the Bavarians' ongoing love of beer today clearly has spiritual origins, and can be seen as having a Bavarian Catholic heritage.

OANS, ZWOA, GSUFFA!

Bavaria's brewing culture was officially born in 1040, when the city of Freising granted the Benedictine abbey brewery in Weihenstephan the right to brew and serve alcoholic beverages. In Munich, too, it was mainly the monasteries which brewed beer professionally some one hundred years after the city's founding in 1158. The monks' beer gained a prominent reputation, for nowhere else was beer produced with such fervour.

To ensure others could also profit from the amber-nectar business, Duke Stephen II established the "brewing constitution" in 1372, and from then on, anyone could purchase "the right to brew" for a fee. But, as one might imagine, this did not always benefit the beer quality; all kinds of preservatives were often added to the brew, making it not only taste terrible, but also at times causing strange psychedelic or other side effects not felt from the monks' cleanly brewed liquid. There was talk of juniper, henbane and bay laurel, of vermouth and poppy juice, and even of ash and ox gall being added. To protect the quality and reputation of his Bavarian beer, Duke William IV of Bavaria finally enacted the "Reinheitsgebot", or the Bavarian Purity Law, in 1516. From then on, Bavarian beer worthy of the name would only consist of barley, hops and water.

To this day, Bavarians still treat their beer as a staple, and are uncompromising in their choice. Once "the one" has been found – and sometimes this is even inherited – they will only frequent establishments which serve "their" beer. The Bavarians' ongoing pride in the spiritual roots of beer is on display every year in Munich at the world's largest beer festival, the Oktoberfest (although it actually starts in September), when the entire city goes wild for 16 whole days. Then it's a question of everyone from all corners of the globe, whether Japan, New Zealand or Australia, donning traditional dirndl and lederhosen costumes and toasting each other "One, two, bottoms up!".

With the first rays of the sun, the Bavarians go outside to a beer garden. Most of them bring their own food – and pickled sausages or sour brawn are always in the basket. You can of course buy both of these as well as various other Brotzeit treats at the snack bars, but they taste so much better if they're made at home.

SAUSAGE SALAD

EASY AND GOOD

SERVES 4:

150 g gherkins (from a jar, with 300 ml gherkin liquid)
1 red onion
2 tbsp white vinegar
100 ml vegetable stock
1 tsp medium-hot mustard
1 tsp sugar
salt | freshly ground black pepper
8 tbsp vegetable oil
500 g Regensburger or Lyoner boiled sausage
1 bunch chives

HOW LONG IT TAKES: c. 20 min
MARINATING: c. 1 hour
PER PORTION: c. 595 kcal | 16 g p | 58 g f | 4 g ch

1 Thinly slice the gherkins. Peel and halve the onion, then cut it into thin strips. In a bowl, combine the gherkin liquid, vinegar, stock, mustard and sugar, using a whisk. Season with salt and pepper. Place the gherkins and the onion into the marinade and stir to combine well, then stir in the oil. Stir everything again, check the seasoning to taste.

2 Pull the skin off the Regensburger or Lyoner sausage, then cut the meat into thin slices or strips. Stir the sausage into the marinade and leave to marinate for at least 1 hour.

3 Rinse the chives, shake dry, then snip into thin rings. Serve the sausage salad in deep plates with a little of the marinade drizzled over the top, then sprinkle with the chives. Serve the salad with pretzels or rye bread with butter.

SOUR "RED-WHITE" PRESSSACK

RUSTIC AND SPICY

SERVES 4:

4 slices each of red and white Presssack (= brawn, weighing 100 g each and c. 1 cm thick)
200 ml beef broth (p.52, or ready-made beef stock)
4 tbsp white vinegar
1 tsp sugar
salt | freshly ground black pepper
4 tbsp vegetable oil
1 large red and 1 large white onion

HOW LONG IT TAKES: c. 10 min
MARINATING: c. 30 min
PER SERVING: c. 310 kcal | 16 g p | 24 g f | 5 g ch

1 If necessary, remove skins or strings from the Presssack slices. Place 1 red and 1 white slice into each deep plate.

2 Warm the beef broth until lukewarm, transfer to a bowl and combine with the vinegar, sugar, salt and pepper. Leave the marinade to stand for 5 minutes until all the spices are dissolved, whisk in the oil.

3 Peel the onions, cut or shave into very thin rings and arrange on the Presssack – white onions on the red Presssack, red onions on the white Presssack. Pour about 7 tablespoons of marinade into each plate and leave to marinate for about 30 minutes. Serve the Presssack with farmhouse bread, pretzels or Brotzeit sticks (p.31).

SOUR CHEESE

SOUR AND AROMATIC

SERVES 4:
150 g gherkins (from a jar, with 200 ml gherkin liquid)
1 large red onion
4 tbsp white vinegar
1 tsp sugar
salt | freshly ground black pepper
400 g Limburger cheese (or Maroilles cheese)
200 g Handkäse (sour milk cheese, plain or blue)
3 tbsp sunflower oil

HOW LONG IT TAKES: c. 15 min
MARINATING: c. 1 hour
PER SERVING: c. 420 kcal | 38 g p | 28 g f | 4 g ch

1 Cut the gherkins into ½ cm cubes. Peel and finely dice the onion. Combine the gherkin liquid with the vinegar and sugar, season with salt and pepper to taste and stir well. Leave the marinade to stand for about 5 minutes until all the spices are dissolved.

2 Cut both types of cheese into 1 cm slices. Stir the oil into the marinade, add the gherkin and onion cubes and stir everything again to combine well. Check and adjust the seasoning with salt and pepper.

3 Put 2–3 tablespoons marinade into a shallow dish (c. 18 x 30 cm). Place the cheese slices into the dish side by side, alternating. Pour over the remaining marinade, cover with clingfilm and leave to draw flavour for at least 1 hour at room temperature.

USEFUL TIPS

The longer you leave the cheese in the liquid, the better will it take on the aroma of the marinade. You can even marinate the cheese a day in advance; in that case omit the onions and add them only just before serving (finely cut them into very thin rings instead of dicing them if you like).
Really delicious: Add 1–2 pinches of caraway seeds to the cheese salad. If you don't like to bite on the seeds, use ground caraway instead.

OBAZDA

Obazda, pronounced "o-buts-dah", cannot simply be translated. A beer garden classic, this well-spiced, mashed-up cheese, butter and cream spread needs to be enjoyed to be understood.

FLAVOURSOME AND CREAMY

SERVES 4–6:

1 small onion
100 g soft butter
120 g ripe Romadur cheese (45 % fat, or any other red culture cheese)
200 g ripe Brie or Camembert
½ tsp sweet paprika
2 pinches of hot paprika
1 tsp caraway seeds
2 tbsp wheat beer (optional)
150 g cream cheese
salt | freshly ground black pepper
1 bunch chives

HOW LONG IT TAKES: c. 25 min
MARINATING: c. 1 hour
PER SERVING (when serving 6):
c. 365 kcal | 16 g p | 33 g f | 1 g ch

1 Peel and finely dice the onion. Melt 1 tablespoon of butter in a frying pan. Add the onion and fry, stirring, for 5 minutes until translucent or golden. Take off the stove and leave to cool.

2 Finely dice the cheese (see tips). In a bowl, beat the remaining butter with the whisks of a handheld mixer for 2 minutes until nice and creamy. Whisk in the diced cheese, paprika, caraway seeds and the wheat beer if using, adding the cream cheese right at the end. Season with salt and pepper to taste, but use the salt only sparingly as the two cheeses are already quite salty.

3 Stir the onion into the beaten cheese mixture, check the seasoning and leave to rest and marinate for at least 1 hour. Just before serving, rinse the chives under cold water, shake dry and snip into thin rings. Place the Obazda in a bowl or on a chopping board, spinkle with the chives – and enjoy.

USEFUL TIPS

The cheese for an Obazda is easiest to work when it is at room temperature, so it pays to remember and take it out of the fridge before making the dish. To chop strong types of cheese such as Romadur or Miesbacher, it's best to wear disposable kitchen gloves and chop the cheese on top of the wrapping paper – this way, neither your hands nor the cutting board will take on the strong cheese aroma.

LIGHT-WEIGHT VARIATION

To serve 4, pull apart 200 g ripe Camembert roughly with your fingers, place into a bowl and combine with 200 g cream cheese. Beat both with the whisks of a handheld mixer for about 2 minutes until creamy. Season with salt, pepper, 1 tsp sweet paprika, a pinch of ground caraway seeds and a pinch of sugar. Spoon this Obazda "light" into 2 screw-top jars (of 200 ml each), close well and keep chilled in the fridge until serving. If you like, you can also place some snipped chives and diced onion on the table (white or red onion) when serving. Now everyone can help themselves and garnish their own Obazda to their own taste.

2012

BEER GARDEN FAVOURITES

Sitting outside under the chestnut trees and idly wondering whether the afternoon sun can penetrate through the leaves while enjoying a freshly drawn half or a whole Mass. This is somehow refreshing, and deeply relaxing for the mind, to the point where it doesn't matter anymore who shares your bench. The beer garden provides a unique opportunity to see the Bavarians, otherwise more likely to be shy with strangers, talk to people from far and distant lands such as Rome or Tokyo, or even Düsseldorf in the Rhineland. This may well be due to the distinctive atmosphere felt in a Bavarian beer garden, rooted in a parallel universe somewhere between zen and social interaction. Or it may simply be the delicious beer ...

The Bavarians owe this traditional and much-loved beer garden institution under the chestnut trees to the long-established Munich breweries. In 1539, new brewing laws stated that beer could only be brewed between the feast days of St Michael (29 September) and St George (23 April). It was prohibited during the hot summer months, because the boiling process created a serious risk of fire. To ensure that customers weren't left high and dry during this "dry" period, the last beer – the so-called Märzenbier, or March beer, – was brewed to be more full-bodied, making it longer lasting, but also more palatable. To tide their stocks of beer over the warmer months, the brewers would set up storage cellars next to their breweries. In winter they would prepare by cutting lots of ice from the surrounding ponds and filling the cellars with it to keep the barrels cool in summer. Leafy horse chestnut trees were also planted to overhang the roofs, their thick foliage providing additional pleasant, cool shade.

PROST MITNAND! – CHEERS EVERYONE!

Under these inviting chestnut trees there was also room for tables and benches – the perfect place for the brewers' Brotzeit, or break time. And gradually, walkers and daytrippers would also join in, enjoying a freshly drawn beer to ease the thirst in the midday heat. But what became a great sideline business for the brewers was an affront for publicans, who were up in arms about their lost business. In order to curb any further derailment, King Maximilian I of Bavaria decreed on 4 January 1812 that, unlike the pubs, the breweries were only able to serve beer, not meals.

So anyone wanting to enjoy a beer under the great chestnut trees now had to bring their own food, though even this could only consist of cold meals and other homemade snacks often packed in a basket. It would all be served on a checked tablecloth – just not one with the Bavarian diamond pattern. Set on the table were wooden cutting boards, and a selection of Bavarian beer radishes and little red radishes, fresh butter, Leberkäse (Bavarian loaf-shaped sausage), Obatzda (mashed cheese spread) or Griebenschmalz (crackling fat). This arrangement marked the official birth of the world-famous Bavarian beer garden. And the cosy spots under the trees – at least in the city – soon became vast stomping grounds for open-air drinkers of all ages, ethnic and new Bavarians, visitors and tourists, who gather here in rare and, above all, democratic harmony.

HOMEMADE LIVER PÂTÉ

This dish was traditionally made by butchers who knew how much meat to use and how to spice the mixture. This recipe is easy to follow and a good start to making pâté at home.

SOME EFFORT, BUT JOLLY GOOD

MAKES 6 JARS:
400 g onions | 3 cloves
3 large and 6 small bay leaves
1 tsp juniper berries | salt
700 g pork belly (important: as fatty as possible!)
300 g pig's liver (cleaned, best to pre-order from the butcher)
80 g butter | 100 g lard
freshly ground black pepper
1 heaped tbsp curing salt (20 g, Prague Powder #1)
1 tsp dried marjoram
½ tsp vanilla sugar (don't be surprised, it counters the bitter taste of the liver)
a pinch of ground allspice
freshly grated nutmeg
Plus: mincer with a 4 mm disc
kitchen thermometer, 6 screw-top jars (200 ml each)

HOW LONG IT TAKES: c. 3 hours 45 min
CHILLING: overnight
PER JAR: c. 635 kcal | 32 g p | 55 g f | 4 g ch

1 Peel the onions, halve one, finely dice the rest. Put 3 litres water, the onion halves, cloves, large bay leaves, juniper berries and 2 tablespoons of salt into a saucepan and bring to the boil. Cut the pork belly into 10 equal pieces, place in the water and simmer uncovered and over low heat for about 1 hour 30 minutes. Roughly chop the liver, cover and chill.

2 Meanwhile melt the butter in a frying pan. Add the diced onion and fry over medium heat for about 18 minutes until golden, take out and leave to cool. Melt the lard in the pan, season with salt and pepper, and take off the stove. Place the screw-top jars and the lids in boiling water, take out the jars and let drip dry. Leave the lids in the water.

3 Drain the pork belly into a sieve, catching the juice and measuring off 200 ml. Season the liver with two-thirds of the pickling salt, combine well and turn through a mincer into a large bowl, constantly stirring the mixture. Mince the pork belly and stir well into the liver. Mince the onion cubes and the reserved cooking liquid and stir into the liver mixture. Season with the remaining spices, vanilla sugar and curing salt. Transfer 400 g of the liver mixture to a second bowl and purée finely with a handheld mixer, then stir back into the remaining mixture.

4 Divide the liver mixture between the jars, hitting them several times onto the work surface in order to remove any air bubbles. Spread the lukewarm lard on top of the liver mixture and place 1 small bay leaf on each one. Close the jars with the lids.

5 Place a trivet in the base of a wide saucepan and arrange the jars on top. Pour in about 1.5 litres of lukewarm water to cover the jars. Position the kitchen thermometer so that it is in the water. Slowly heat everything to a temperature of 80–85°C, cook the liver mixture for 1 hour 30 minutes. Take the jars out of the saucepan, leave them to cool, then chill overnight. Remove the liver pâté from the fridge about 30 minutes before serving. Tastes delicious on farmhouse bread with pickled gherkins or mustard.

PORK DRIPPINGS

YUMMY AND INEXPENSIVE

SERVES 4–6:

1 large onion
200 g pork dripping (e.g. the fat skimmed off the pork knuckle on p.73)
2 pinches of caraway seeds
2 pinches of dried marjoram
salt | freshly ground black pepper
a few slices rye bread

HOW LONG IT TAKES: c. 20 min
CHILLING: overnight
PER SERVING (when serving 6):
c. 415 kcal | 4 g p | 34 g f | 22 g ch

1 Peel and finely dice the onion. Put 2 tablespoons pork drippings into a frying pan and melt. Add the diced onions and fry over medium heat for 6–7 minutes until golden. Add another 1 tablespoon of fat and fry the onion for a further 2 minutes.

2 Season the onion with the caraway seeds and the marjoram, add the remaining pork drippings and heat through. Reduce the temperature and allow everything to simmer gently over low heat for about 2 minutes. Generously season the fat with salt and plenty of pepper.

3 Pour the hot drippings into a heatproof jar or into individual dishes, close or cover. Leave the drippings to cool, then chill in the fridge overnight.

4 To serve, either spread the drippings thickly onto slices of bread and serve these at the table, or serve the bread in a basket and offer the fat in a jar or in the individual dishes for everyone to spread onto their bread slices themselves.

ROAST PORK BRAWN

Pork roast does not lend itself to reheating, but it's all the more delicious cold – whether as a Brotzeit sack with freshly grated horseradish or as a tasty Bratensulz, as in this recipe.

LOOKS PRETTY TOO

SERVES 4:

¾ l beef broth (p.52, but unspiced, or ready-made beef stock)
1 sachet aspic powder (25 g, see tips)
6 tbsp white wine vinegar
salt | sugar
4 eggs (medium) | 4 gherkins
150 g cherry tomatoes (if liked)
500 g cold roast pork (e.g. neck of pork, p.71, or pork knuckle, p.73)

HOW LONG IT TAKES: c. 40 min
CHILLING: c. 4 hours
PER SERVING: c. 415 kcal | 41 g p | 22 g f | 6 g ch

1 In a saucepan, bring the beef broth to the boil, working in the aspic powder according to the packet instructions. Season the brawn with vinegar, salt and sugar (see tips and info), leave to cool and skim if necessary.

2 Put the eggs into boiling water, cook for about 10 minutes until hard-boiled, drain, rinse under cold water, shell and cut into thin slices. Cut the gherkins diagonally into thin slices. Wash the tomatoes, if necessary, and halve them. Cut the roast pork into 8 slices (c. 1 cm thick).

3 Divide the roast pork, eggs, gherkins and cherry tomatoes between deep plates, then pour over the brawn liquid. Make sure everything is well covered and "submersed". Cover with clingfilm and chill for at least 4 hours (even better overnight).

USEFUL TIPS

If you have no aspic powder at home, you can use 9 sheets of white gelatin instead. Soak the gelatin in cold water 5–10 minutes, lightly squeeze out, add to the hot beef broth and stir briefly. The gelatin will quickly dissolve. Season the liquid brawn and continue as described in the recipe. The aspic powder is, however, more aromatic as it has been seasoned with spices, celery and carrots. Important: Make sure you generously season the brawn liquid, using lots of vinegar and spices, perhaps even over-seasoning it, so that it almost takes your breath away. This is necessary because the ingredients (here meat, eggs, gherkin and tomatoes) will absorb plenty of the liquid's flavour after after it has cooled and set.

WHAT IS BRAWN?

You can make savoury brawns using vegetables, meat and fish. Sweet jellies also taste delicious. Whether savoury or sweet, you will always need the so-called jelly stock, that is a well-seasoned liquid which sets after cooling. Fish, vegetable or beef broths are used as a basis for savoury brawns; for the sweet variation, a mixture of wine or sparkling wine and sugar syrup may be used, or alternatively alcohol-free apple, grape or redcurrant juice. The resulting liquid is then thickened with aspic powder, leaf or powder gelatin – it jellifies and the brawn thus achieves its typical consistency. For a vegetarian variation of the basic brawn recipe you can use non-meat jellifying agents, such as agar or locust bean gum flour (these are made from algae and seed pods and are available in most health food stores).

BROTZEIT STICKS

Bavarians love bread, especially dark country bread, and bread rolls – with or without seeds. There is an enormous variety of ways to make it, and they have the most poetic names: Pfennigmuckerl, Sternsemmeln, Mohnstangerl or, as here: Brotzeitstangerl.

CRUNCHY AND SPICY

MAKES 12 STICKS:

250 g rye flour (for sourdough bread)
250 g wheat flour (pastry flour)
½ tsp fennel seeds
½ tsp coriander seeds
1 ½ tsp salt
1 cube fresh yeast (42 g)
1 tsp sugar
1 tsp caraway seeds
1 level tsp coarse sea salt (lightly crushed with pestle and mortar, depending on the size of the grains)
flour for working | baking paper

HOW LONG IT TAKES: c. 30 min
RISING: c. 2 hours
BAKING: c. 40 min
PER STICK: c. 145 kcal | 4 g p | 0 g f | 31 g ch

1 Put the flours into the bowl of your blender (or into a kneading bowl if you are using a handheld blender). Finely crush the fennel and coriander seeds with pestle and mortar, then stir with the salt into the flour. Crumble the yeast into a cup, add 5 tablespoons of lukewarm water, 1 tablespoon of flour (from the flour mixture in the bowl) and the sugar. Stir to combine. Add to the flour in the bowl, together with 300 ml lukewarm water, and knead everything with the kneading hooks of the blender – start at a slow speed until all ingredients are well combined, then knead for 5 minutes on a high speed. Put a little flour into the bowl so that the dough comes away from the sides, and knead for another 1–2 minutes.

2 Transfer the dough to a lightly floured work surface, hand-knead for another 2–3 minutes and shape into a ball. Dust the bottom of the bowl with flour, put the dough ball into the bowl, cover with a kitchen cloth and leave to rise in a warm place for 40 minutes. Knead again the dough in the bowl and leave to rise for another 1 hour.

3 Line two baking trays with baking paper. Transfer the dough to the floured work surface, shape it into a thick roll and divide this into 12 same-sized pieces (c. 70 g). Shape the dough pieces into 16–17 cm long sticks and place on the baking trays without touching each other. With a knife, make three diagonal cuts into the upper sides of each stick, cover them and leave to rest for another 20 minutes. Preheat the oven to 210°C (convection oven 190°C).

4 Lightly brush the sticks with cold water, then sprinkle with caraway seeds and sea salt. Put both baking trays into the oven – one top, one bottom – and bake the sticks for about 40 minutes until they are golden brown and crisp. If your oven uses top and bottom heat, swap the trays over after about 25 minutes. This ensures that the sticks will be evenly baked. In a convection oven the heat will circulate and the trays do not have to be swapped.

5 Take the finished bread sticks out of the oven, place on a cooling rack and leave to cool. Eat soon so the sticks will still be crisp and fresh.

DUMPLINGS WITH ALPINE CHEESE

Bavarian cuisine is famous for its dumplings, which make ideal companions for roast pork, roast goose and goulash. They are also really good on their own – for example in a sour dressing with alpine cheese and radishes.

SUMMERY AND FRESH

SERVES 4:

300 ml vegetable stock (ready-made stock or homemade stock, see right)
6 tbsp white wine vinegar
1½ tsp sugar
salt | freshly ground black pepper
6 tbsp vegetable oil
500 g cold bread or serviette dumplings (pp.89 or 90)
200 g mild alpine cheese (thinly sliced)
½ bunch radishes
1 bunch chives

HOW LONG IT TAKES: c. 20 min
PER SERVING: c. 610 kcal | 24 g p | 38 g f | 42 g ch

1 Heat the vegetable stock to lukewarm, transfer to a bowl, stir in the vinegar, sugar, salt and pepper. Leave the marinade to stand for 5 minutes until the spices are dissolved, then whisk in the oil.

2 Meanwhile, cut the dumplings into ½ cm slices and place them into a shallow dish. Cut the cheese into strips about 1 cm wide. Wash, trim and thinly slice or shave the radishes. Arrange the radishes and cheese on the dumpling slices, pour over and gently combine with the marinade, then leave to absorb the flavour for about 5 minutes.

3 Rinse the chives and shake dry. Snip them into thin rings and sprinkle over the dumpling salad just before serving.

USEFUL AND VERY VERSATILE: A HOMEMADE VEGETABLE STOCK

To make 2 litres of basic vegetable stock, wash or peel, trim and roughly chop 150 g onions, 150 g celeriac, 200 g celery, 200 g carrots, 100 g parsley roots and 200 g tomatoes. Peel and halve 1 garlic clove. Cut 1 leek (c. 100 g) lengthways and wash thoroughly. In a wide saucepan, heat 2 tbsp olive oil. Add the onions, celeriac, carrots and parsley roots and sauté for about 5 minutes. Season with 2 pinches of salt. Add the celery, tomatoes, garlic and 1 tablespoon of dried button mushrooms, pour in 2.5 litres water and bring to the boil. Simmer the stock over low heat for about 45 minutes. Now rinse a few parsly sprigs and add together with the leek, ½ teaspoon juniper berries, 1 teaspoon black peppercorns, 2 bay leaves and ½ teaspoon allspice berries. Cook for another 45 minutes. Pour the vegetable stock through a fine sieve (if possible, use a sieve that you have lined with a fine straining cloth or kitchen towel), catching the stock. Discard the vegetables and immediately use the stock. Alternatively, pour the stock into thoroughly cleaned screw-top jars, close them well and place them upside down to cool. You can of course also fill the stock into suitable freezer containers and freeze it for future use.

BAVARIAN BURGERS

A Fleischpflanzerl, or Bavarian burger, should be light, aromatic, juicy and crunchy. The soaked bread roll makes it light, mustard and spices supply flavour, and if well cooked it will be juicy and crunchy.

IRRESISTIBLE COLD OR HOT

SERVES 4:

2 stale bread rolls (c. 100 g)
150 ml milk
1 large onion
1 small garlic clove
6–8 sprigs flat-leaved parsley
2 tbsp butter
salt | 2 eggs (large)
500 g mixed minced meat (pork and beef)
1 tbsp medium-hot mustard
1 tbsp coarse-grained mustard
2 tbsp breadcrumbs
freshly ground black pepper
2 pinches cayenne pepper
2 tbsp clarified butter

HOW LONG IT TAKES: c. 30 min
RESTING: c. 10 min
IN THE OVEN: c. 20 min
PER SERVING: c. 570 kcal | 33 g p | 39 g f | 21 g ch

1 Cut the bread rolls into 1 cm dice and place them in a bowl. Heat the milk to lukewarm and pour evenly over the breadroll dice. Peel and finely dice the onion and the garlic. Rinse and shake dry the parsley, pull off the leaves and chop, but not too finely.

2 In a small saucepan heat the butter until it starts to foam, then use a little of the butter to brush a baking tray. Add the onion and garlic dice to the saucepan with the remaining butter and cook over low heat for about 5 minutes until translucent. Lightly season with salt and leave to cool.

3 Combine the soaked bread rolls with the eggs, onion, garlic, parsley, minced meat, the two types of mustard and the breadcrumbs. Season to taste with salt, pepper and cayenne pepper. Leave the mince mixture to swell for 10 minutes.

4 Preheat the oven to 140°C (convection oven 120°C). Divide the mince mixture into 12 even portions. With moistened hands, shape each portion into a ball and flatten slightly.

5 In a large frying pan, melt the clarified butter. Add the burgers and fry for 2 minutes until golden brown, turn and fry the other side for 2 minutes until also golden brown. Transfer the burgers from the frying pan to a baking tray, put into the oven (centre) and continue cooking for 20 minutes until finished.

6 Remove the burgers from the oven and arrange on warm plates. A potato salad (pp.44/45) makes for an excellent accompaniment.

USEFUL TIPS

Finishing the burgers in the oven means they will stay nice and juicy. Of course you can also cook them in the frying pan until they are done: Simply start by frying the burgers as described, then cover and finish cooking over low heat for 15 minutes, turning them several times.

The burgers taste even better and more "classy" if you make them with minced veal. And if you still have some homemade sauce (e.g. from the roast pork or the dark sauce, pp.71 and 76), the simple burgers will become a veritable feast.

STEAK TARTARE AND CHIVE SANDWICH

The old-fashioned way of presenting a steak tartare is to put the raw, minced beef in the middle of the plate, top it with an egg yolk and garnish it with onions and gherkins. Everyone can see the fresh meat and then dress their own tartare to taste at the table. This delicious variation is ready-made for you to enjoy.

EXTRAVAGANT AND SPICY

SERVES 4:

For the tartare:

2 shallots
3 anchovy fillets (in oil)
1 tsp capers (in brine)
2 gherkins
500 g minced beef (freshly minced by the butcher)
2 egg yolks (medium)
1 tsp medium-hot mustard
1 tsp hot mustard
a few dashes of Tabasco
salt | freshly ground black pepper

For the chive sandwiches:

1–2 bunches chives
4–8 slices country bread (depending on size)
butter for spreading

HOW LONG IT TAKES: c. 15 min
PER SERVING: c. 550 kcal | 37 g p | 29 g f | 35 g ch

1 To make the tartare, peel and finely dice the shallots. Rinse the anchovy fillets under cold water, then pat them dry and finely chop them. Drain, pat dry and finely chop the capers. Also cut the gherkins into small dice.

2 Put the minced beef into a large bowl. Add the shallots, anchovy fillets, capers, gherkins, egg yolks and both types of mustard, then gently combine everything until well mixed. Season generously to taste with Tabasco, salt and pepper.

3 To make the sandwiches, rinse the chives under cold water, shake dry and snip into thin rings. Evenly spread the chives on a shallow plate. Thickly spread the bread slices with butter, then leave whole or halve depending on their size. Press the buttered bread slices butter side down into the chives.

4 Arrange the beef tartare on plates and serve with the open chive sandwiches.

OR TRY THIS: MEDIUM RARE STEAK TARTARE

Roll the prepared tartare with moistened hands to form 8 even-sized balls, then flatten them slightly to form steaks. In each of two large frying pans, heat 2 tablespoons of vegetable oil. Put 4 steaks into each pan, fry over medium heat for 2 minutes, turn, fry for another 1 minute. Take the pan off the heat and leave the steaks to finish cooking for another 1 minute until medium rare. Goes well with boiled buttery potatoes, a green salad and golden-fried onion rings.

USEFUL TIPS

To make beef tartare, only the tenderest meat free from sinews is used, for example fillet of beef. Gourmets do not put the meat through a mincer but, cut it into very fine dice using a sharp knife. Mustard, Tabasco, salt and pepper supply the basic seasoning of the tartare. If you want to add another flavour note, why not try using 2 tablespoons of a spicy tomato ketchup and a few dashes of Worcestershire sauce?

0,5l
rastal

0,5 l
rastal

TIME FOR A WHITE SAUSAGE!

When it comes to sausages, Bavarian butchery can boast a truly incomparable array. The most famous Bavarian sausage, so the story goes, was fittingly created at the "Ewigen Licht" (Eternal Light) inn at Munich's Marienplatz, where the Weisswurst (Bavarian white sausage) was invented by accident by butcher Josef Moser. In the early hours of Carnival Sunday 1857, he was rolling his tasty veal sausage as per usual, when he soon noticed he had run out of sheep casings. In his desperation – the first patrons had already started arriving – he simply stuffed the sausage meat into pig intestines, twisted the ends, and boiled the sausages in hot water. The Weisswurst was a huge success, conquering the whole of Bavaria – and transformed the "Main Line" (the tacit line between northern and southern Germany formed by the river Main) into the "Weisswurst Equator", which, for Bavarians, marks the start of foreign territory.

The Weisswurst is said to be even older than the sausage invented by Josef Moser. An engraving from 1814 depicts some locals sucking on Weisswürste in the Bockkeller beer hall – one of the original forms of eating the sausages, in which the meat is gradually "drawn" (sucked) out of the casing using one's teeth. The reigning "Weisswurst King", who has won the title several times, actually comes from Baden-Württemberg, but at least he is a member of the "Association for the Protection of Munich White Sausages".

TIME'S UP, IT'S PAST TWELVE!

The rule that white sausages should never hear the church bells toll twelve dates back to the time when, due to the lack of modern cooling equipment, they had to be boiled shortly after production to ensure they did not spoil. Today, thanks to refrigerators (and preservatives), exceptions are tolerated. The white sausage is placed in hot water before serving, and is eaten warm and – always! – without the skin.

There are many ways to eat white sausages properly, apart from sucking. A good option for beginners is the "Längsschnitt", or lengthways cut, where the sausage is sliced down the middle, without being totally severed in two. Both sides are then folded back, and the meat scooped out. The "Kreuzschnitt", or crossways cut, is for the nimble-fingered: the sausage is held in place with a fork and a diagonal incision made about 4 cm from one end. The filling is then scooped out, and the process continued in a zigzag pattern all the way down. It should be accompanied by sweet mustard, fresh pretzels and a fresh wheat beer. That's the only way it will make you happy and ensure a relaxing wind-down to your day. Because, as the saying goes, "He who eats Weisswurst in the morning will not fight at night!"

There are many types of radish: large and small, longish and round, red, white and two-coloured. A root vegetable with a slightly peppery taste, it is often served raw in a salad or by itself. Salt is an absolute must to bring out the best flavour in these healthy, vitamin-packed crunchers.

RADISH SALAD

SUMMERY AND FRESH

SERVES 4:

2 bunches radishes (c. 350 g each)
salt
4 tbsp white wine vinegar
1 tsp brown sugar
4 tbsp vegetable oil
1 small bunch chives

HOW LONG IT TAKES: c. 15 min
MARINATING: c. 35 min
PER SERVING: c. 115 kcal | 2 g p | 10 g f | 4 g ch

1 Wash the radishes, cut off and discard the roots and green parts. Cut or shave the radishes into thin slices and put them into a bowl. Season with salt, stir to combine and leave to stand for 20 minutes.

2 Stir together the white wine vinegar and the sugar, leave to stand briefly, then whisk in the oil. Put the radishes into a sieve, add the liquid drained from them to the dressing, and leave to stand for another 15 minutes.

3 Rinse and shake dry the chives, then snip them into thin rings. Just before serving, stir the chives into the radish salad and check the seasoning.

BAVARIAN BEER RADISH SALAD

BAVARIAN HOT STUFF

SERVES 4:

2 long beer radishes (c. 450 g each)
salt
2 tbsp white vinegar
2 tbsp white wine vinegar
a pinch of sugar
freshly ground black pepper
4 tbsp sunflower oil
2 sprigs flat-leaved parsley (if liked)

HOW LONG IT TAKES: c. 15 min
MARINATING: c. 35 min
PER SERVING: c. 120 kcal | 2 g p | 10 g f | 5 g ch

1 Remove the roots and the green parts, then peel the radishes. Cut or shave the radishes into thin strips, put them into a bowl, season with salt and stir well to combine. Leave to stand for just under 20 minutes.

2 Stir together both types of vinegar with the sugar and the pepper. Leave to stand for a little while, then whisk in the oil. Put the radishes into a sieve and add the liquid drained from them to the dressing and leave to marinate for another 15 minutes.

3 Rinse the parsley if necessary and shake or pat dry. Pull off and chop the leaves. Check the seasoning of the radish salad, add some parsley if liked, serve and enjoy.

POTATO AND ENDIVE SALAD

NICELY SPICED AND GOOD-LOOKING

SERVES 4:

1kg salad potatoes
salt | 1 small onion
80g smoked streaky bacon, without rind
3½tbsp vegetable oil
100g curly endive salad leaves
200ml beef stock (p.52, or ready-made beef stock)
4tbsp white vinegar
2tsp medium-hot mustard
freshly ground black pepper
2 pinches of sugar

HOW LONG IT TAKES: c. 50 min
PER SERVING: c. 380 kcal | 9g p | 23g f | 32g ch

1 Wash the potatoes, boil them in plenty of salted water for about 20 minutes until done, then drain. Briefly leave to cool, then slip of the skins and cut the potatoes into ½ cm thick slices. Put the potato slices into a bowl.

2 Meanwhile, peel the onion; finely dice onion and bacon. Put the bacon into a frying pan with ½ tablespoon oil and fry the bacon for 3 minutes over medium heat. Add the onion and fry for a further 3 minutes. Take off the stove. Wash and shake dry the curly endive leaves, stack the leaves on top of each other and cut them into strips.

3 Heat the beef stock and stir in the vinegar, mustard, salt, pepper and sugar. Pour the dressing over the potato slices and leave to marinate for 5 minutes. Add the onion and bacon mixture and the remaining oil, combine well, sprinkle with the endive strips and carefully stir again. Check the seasoning, then serve the potato salad lukewarm.

USEFUL TIP

Only add the oil to the salad right at the end. First the potatoes need to absorb plenty of the stock – for a really good potato salad needs to be shiny and under no circumstances should it be dry.

BASIC POTATO SALAD

CLASSIC AND GOOD

SERVES 4:

1 kg salad potatoes (e.g. Charlotte)
salt
1 tsp caraway seeds
1 large onion
2 tbsp butter
freshly ground black pepper
1 bunch flat-leaved parsley
200 ml beef broth (p.52, or ready-made beef stock)
4 tbsp white vinegar
2 pinches of sugar
4 tbsp vegetable oil

HOW LONG IT TAKES: c. 45 min
PER SERVING: c. 305 kcal | 7 g p | 15 g f | 32 g ch

1 Wash the potatoes, then boil in plenty of salted water with the caraway seeds for about 20 minutes until done. Drain, briefly leave to cool, peel, then cut into ½ cm thick slices. Put into a bowl.

2 Meanwhile, peel and finely dice the onion. Put the butter into a frying pan to melt, add the onion and fry for about 5 minutes over medium heat until translucent. Season with salt and pepper and take off the stove. Rinse and shake dry the parsley, pull off and roughly chop the leaves.

3 Add the onion to the potatoes. Heat the stock and stir in the vinegar, salt, pepper and sugar. Pour the dressing over the potato slices, leave to stand for 5 minutes. Add the oil and carefully stir to combine well. Check and adjust the seasoning to taste, add the parsley and serve.

POTATO AND CUCUMBER SALAD

BAVARIA'S FAVOURITE

SERVES 4:

1 kg salad potatoes (e.g. Jersey Royals)
salt
1 small cucumber (c. 400 g)
200 ml beef broth (p.52, or ready-made beef stock)
4 tbsp white wine vinegar
freshly ground black pepper
2 pinches of sugar
4 tbsp vegetable oil

HOW LONG IT TAKES: c. 45 min
PER SERVING: c. 270 kcal | 7 g p | 11 g f | 32 g ch

1 Wash the potatoes, then boil them in plenty of salted water for about 20 minutes until done. Drain and briefly leave to cool. Peel and cut into ½ cm thick slices. Put into a bowl.

2 Meanwhile, wash the cucumber and peel it so that green strips of peel remain. Shave the cucumber into thin slices, place them into a bowl, season lightly with salt and leave to stand for 10 minutes. Put the cucumber into a sieve and squeeze out.

3 Heat the beef stock, then stir in the vinegar, salt, pepper and sugar. Pour the dressing over the potatoes, leave to stand for 5 minutes. Add the oil and combine well. Add the cucumber slices, and stir again. Check the seasoning and serve lukewarm.

THERE'S NO TASTE LIKE HOME

What's for lunch? Whether it's a hot beef broth or a crispy Bavarian pork roast, whatever the Bavarians cook up in their kitchens they can be rightly proud of – it's always delicious. And unlike anything served in any tavern around the world ...

POTATO SOUP

In the autumn and especially in the winter, a warming soup or a hearty stew is something you can really look forward to. And what could be better than this creamy potato soup, enjoyed steaming hot? If you like, serve it with a smoked eel for a particularly aromatic flavour.

SOOTHINGLY GOOD

SERVES 4–6:

500 g floury potatoes
1 carrot
1 piece celeriac (c. 150 g)
1 large onion
3 tbsp vegetable oil
1.2 l beef broth (p.52, or ready-made beef stock)
1 small leek (c. 50 g)
100 g cream
2 tbsp butter
salt | freshly ground black pepper
freshly grated nutmeg
2 pinches dried marjoram

HOW LONG IT TAKES: c. 25 min
IN THE SAUCEPAN: c. 30 min
PER SERVING (when serving 6):
c. 285 kcal | 12 g p | 17 g f | 12 g ch

1 Wash and peel the potatoes, carrot and celeriac, then cut the vegetables into 1 cm dice. Peel and finely dice the onion.

2 In a saucepan, heat the vegetable oil. Add the onion and sauté for about 3 minutes until it is translucent. Add the vegetable and potato dice and sauté for 1 minute. Pour in the beef broth, bring to the boil and simmer uncovered for about 20 minutes over low heat.

3 Wash and trim the leek, then cut it into ½ cm diamonds or squares. Using a handheld blender, purée the potato soup; not too fine, it's good to have a few chunks left in the soup. Add the leek and cook for 1 minute. Stir in the cream and the butter, then leave the soup to simmer for another 6–7 minutes until nice and creamy.

4 Now, and not before, season the potato soup with salt, pepper, nutmeg and marjoram, check for taste. Serve with farmhouse bread and butter.

OR TRY THIS: POTATO SOUP WITH EEL

Place a 200–250 g smoked eel onto an ovenproof dish and put it into the oven preheated to 100°C (centre; use top and bottom heat, convection is not recommended for this dish). Warm the eel for about 6–8 minutes. Take the fish out of the oven, pull off the skin, carefully separate the flesh from the bones, then tear the fish into bite-sized pieces. Place the eel chunks into warm soup plates or bowls and pour over the hot potato soup.

USEFUL TIPS

If you are serving this soup as a main course dish, it will be sufficient for 4 people. If you offer the soup as an entrée between starter and main course, it will serve 6.
Particularly good: top the soup with a few roasted chanterelle or cep mushrooms.

HOT BEEF BROTH

The classic broth. Whether you use it as a delicious soup or as the basis for a sauce, a hearty meat broth is very versatile in the kitchen. It keeps well and so it's well worth making a large quantity so that you always have some on hand.

WARMS AND NOURISHES

MAKES ABOUT 2 LITRES OF BROTH:

1.2 kg beef brisket
salt | freshly ground black pepper
2 large onions | 2 tbsp vegetable oil
3 marrowbones | 1 large carrot
1 piece celeriac (c. 150 g)
1 parsley root | 1 large tomato
1 leek (c. 60 g) | 1 garlic clove
5 parsley stems (without the leaves!)
2 bay leaves | ½ tsp juniper berries
1 tsp black peppercorns
½ tsp allspice berries
freshly grated nutmeg

HOW LONG IT TAKES: c. 35 min
IN THE SAUCEPAN: c. 4 hours
PER SERVING: c. 1040 kcal | 97 g p | 41 g f | 0 g ch

1 Pat the meat dry and season it with salt and pepper. Wash the onions and halve them without removing the peel. Heat the oil in a large frying pan. Place the onions cut side down into the pan with the meat, then fry both for about 3 minutes. In the last minute, repeatedly turn the meat so that it will be browned all over.

2 Wash the bones and place them with the meat into a narrow tall saucepan. Add 4 litres hot water, bring to the boil and boil rapidly for 5 minutes. Repeatedly skim off any scum that rises to the surface. Turn the heat down and leave to simmer for 1 hour 30 minutes.

3 Wash the vegetables and trim or peel, then halve lengthways. Wash the garlic, rinse the parsley stems. Add all the prepared ingredients and the roasted onions to the saucepan with the spices. Leave everything to simmer for a further 2 hours–2 hours and 30 minutes, until the meat is well cooked.

4 The cooking time will vary according to the quality of the brisket, so it is important to check early on and repeatedly. To check whether the brisket is cooked: pierce the meat with a meat fork. If it is nice and soft, the fork can easily be pulled out of the meat again. Lift the soft, tender meat out of the broth and use as desired (see tip).

5 Pour the broth, a ladle at a time, through a fine sieve (if possible lined with damp straining cloth or a kitchen towel), catching the broth. Use the broth as liked (see tip), seasoning it again with salt, pepper and nutmeg.

USEFUL TIP

Slice the brisket and serve with pumpkin, turnips, potatoes and fresh horseradish (p.82). Peel and finely chop carrot and celeriac and serve in the broth. Other delicious accompaniments to put into your soup are semolina dumplings (p.54), liver dumplings (p.55) or soup noodles.

If you like, you can also scoop the remaining marrow out of the bones and spread it onto lightly toasted farmhouse bread for an evening snack. Season generously to taste with salt and pepper. Discard what you don't use of the marrow.

SEMOLINA GNOCCHI SOUP

CHILDREN LOVE IT TOO

SERVES 4:
50g soft butter | 1 egg yolk (medium)
1 egg (medium) | 100g durum wheat semolina
salt | freshly grated nutmeg
1tsp beef stock granules (optional)
1l beef broth (p.52, or ready-made beef stock)
freshly ground pepper | 1 bunch chives

HOW LONG IT TAKES: c. 25 min
CHILLING: c. 30 min
IN THE SAUCEPAN: c. 30 min
PER SERVING: c. 345 kcal | 18g p | 19g f | 18g ch

1 Beat the butter with the kneading hooks of a handheld mixer for about 3 minutes until white and foaming. Add the egg yolk, stir briefly, then stir in the egg and continue beating. Sprinkle in the semonlina, beat for another 1 minute. Season with 2 pinches each of salt and nutmeg. Cover and leave in a cool place to swell for about 30 minutes.

2 In a large, wide saucepan, bring about 2.5 litres water to the boil, together with 1 teaspoon salt and the stock granules if using.

3 Briefly knead the semolina mixture with your hands. Then, using two teaspoons, shape the semolina mixture into gnocchi (about 20 gnocchi) and slip them into the boiling water. Repeatedly dunk the spoons into hot water so that the mixture will come away from them more easily. Bring the water to the boil again. As soon as all the gnocchi float to the top, cover with the lid at a slant. Simmer the gnocchi over low heat for about 30 minutes.

4 Bring the beef broth to the boil, season with salt and pepper. Rinse and shake dry the chives, then snip into thin rings. Rub a little nutmeg into warm deep plates. Lift the gnocchi out of the water using a slotted spoon and divide them evenly between the plates. Pour over the beef broth, sprinkle with the chives and serve.

LIVER DUMPLING SOUP

This is such a tasty soup, no one will be able to resist. As we say here in Bavaria: a soup without something in it is like a man without strapping legs. So, enjoy your soup!

HERBY AND SPICY

SERVES 8:

150 g day-old bread rolls, cut into slices or large cubes
80 ml milk | 1 large onion
1 garlic clove | 80 g butter
6–8 sprigs flat-leaved parsley
1 small sprig lovage (optional)
2 eggs (medium)
500 g minced beef liver (see tip)
salt | freshly ground black pepper
freshly grated nutmeg
finely grated zest of ½ organic lemon
2 pinches of dried marjoram
30 g breadcrumbs
1 tsp beef stock granules (optional)
2 l beef broth (p.52, or ready-made beef stock)
1 bunch chives

HOW LONG IT TAKES: c. 35 min
CHILLING: c. 30 min
IN THE SAUCEPAN: c. 30 min
PER SERVING: c. 375 kcal | 29 g p | 18 g f | 16 g ch

1 Put the bread slices into a large bowl. Heat the milk to lukewarm and pour evenly over the bread. Set aside and leave to soak. Peel and finely dice the onion and the garlic. Melt the butter in a frying pan. Add the onion and garlic cubes and sauté for about 4 minutes until translucent, take the pan off the stove and leave to cool. Rinse and shake dry the parsley and the lovage, if using, pull off and finely chop the leaves.

2 Put the onion and garlic butter and the herbs, eggs and minced beef liver into the bowl with the bread slices. With your hands or the kneading hook of a handheld mixer, work everything into a smooth mixture. Generously season with salt, pepper, nutmeg, lemon zest and marjoram. Cover and place in the fridge to rest for about 20 minutes. Now work the breadcrumbs into the mixture and return to the fridge to swell for another 10 minutes.

3 In a tall, wide saucepan, bring about 2.5 litres water to the boil with 1 teaspoon salt and the beef stock granules if using.

4 Briefly knead the liver mixture with your hands, then, with moistened hands, shape into 8 even-sized dumplings and place into the boiling water. Bring the water to the boil again. As soon as all the dumplings float to the top, cover the saucepan with the lid at an angle and simmer the dumplings over low heat for about 30 minutes.

5 Bring the beef broth to the boil, season with salt and pepper. Rinse and shake dry the chives, then snip into thin rings. Rub a little nutmeg into the bottom of the warm deep plates. Using a slotted spoon, lift the dumpings out of the water and divide them between the plates. Pour over the beef broth, sprinkle with the chives and serve.

USEFUL TIP

Ask the butcher to prepare and clean the beef liver for liver dumplings. Usually, the beef spleen will also be minced.

A REALLY GOOD CHICKEN SOUP

A hot chicken soup gives you new strength and vital energy. And on some days, our rich noodle soup will even work wonders.

SHEER BLISS, NOT JUST FOR BAVARIANS

SERVES 4:

1 large chicken (c. 1.4 kg) | salt
1 tbsp vegetable or chicken stock granules
1 large carrot
1 leek (c. 100 g)
1 large tomato
1 piece celeriac (c. 200 g)
1 large onion
8 juniper berries
8 allspice berries
1 tsp black peppercorns
2 bay leaves
6 parsley stems (without the leaves!)
3 sprigs lovage (optional)
freshly ground black pepper
freshly grated nutmeg (optional)
½ bunch chives
250 g soup noodles (e.g. vermicelli, alphabet or star pasta)

HOW LONG IT TAKES: c. 1 hour
IN THE SAUCEPAN: c. 3 hours 45 min
PER SERVING: c. 915 kcal | 57 g p | 54 g f | 50 g ch

1 Wash the chicken inside and out, then pat it dry. Halve the chicken first lengthways, then halve the two halves again crossways. Place the chicken pieces into a wide, tall saucepan. Add 3.5 l cold water and season with 1 tablespoon of salt and the stock granules. Bring everything to the boil. Lift out and discard the scum that forms on the surface with a slotted spoon until the liquid is clear. Cook the broth for about 1 hour over medium heat.

2 Peel or wash and trim the vegetables. Halve the carrot, leek and tomato, cut the celeriac into large chunks. Wash and halve the onion, then place it with the skin in a frying pan without fat and dry-fry for about 5 minutes until dark. Put everything with the spices into the saucepan. Rinse the parsley stems and the lovage if using and add to the saucepan. Cook the soup for a further 2 hours 45 minutes.

3 When the soup is cooked, strain it, a little at a time, through a fine sieve, catching the liquid. Leave the chicken to cool, then separate the fatty parts and the bones and discard. Pull the meat into bite-sized pieces. Dice or thinly slice the celeriac and the carrot. Discard the remaining vegetables in the sieve.

4 To make the noodle soup, heat 1 litre of chicken broth (use the rest for other recipes, see tip) with the chicken pieces, celeriac and carrot. Season with salt, pepper and nutmeg, if using, keep warm. Rinse and shake dry the chives and snip into thin rings.

5 Cook the noodles in the boiling salted water according to the packet instructions. Drain in a sieve and divide between warm deep plates. Pour over the broth together with the meat and vegetables, sprinkle with the chives and serve.

USEFUL TIP

This broth is made according to the motto that you can only get something good, if you start off with good ingredients – one part of the soup is used for a tasty soup, the rest can be used for other purposes (for example, a root vegetable soup, p.102).

STUFFED CABBAGE LEAVES WITH HERBS

Good-quality minced meat is wrapped into tender cabbage leaves and then braised in a sauce flavoured with caraway seeds and marjoram – so that everything stays wonderfully juicy and incredibly delicious.

WORTH THE EFFORT

SERVES 4:

1 quantity Bavarian burgers (p.34)
1½ tsp dried marjoram
8 large pointed cabbage leaves (c. 400 g)
salt
200 g onions
1 tbsp clarified butter
½ tsp tomato purée
1 heaped tsp flour
600 ml meat stock (from a jar, or water or beef broth, p.52)
1 tsp caraway seeds
4 rashers bacon (c. 80 g)
1 tsp vegetable oil
1 tsp cold butter
freshly ground black pepper
Plus: kitchen twine

HOW LONG IT TAKES: c. 50 min
IN THE OVEN: c. 1 hour 30 min
PER SERVING: c. 1120 kcal | 44 g p | 93 g f | 27 g ch

1 Prepare the burger mixture as described on p.34, with additional marjoram seasoning.

2 Wash the pointed cabbage leaves. In a wide saucepan, bring plenty of water to the boil, adding plenty of salt. Place the cabbage leaves into the water, push under and cook for 2 minutes. Lift the cabbage leaves out of the water and immediately rinse under cold water, spread them out on kitchen paper and pat dry.

3 For each cabbage leaf, cut off the top of the central rib to flatten. Place 2 cabbage leaves next to each other, overlapping and spread a quarter of the meat mixture onto each pair. Fold the long sides of the cabbage leaves over the filling, then tightly roll up the cabbage leaves from their narrow ends. Using kitchen twine, tightly tie up each parcel.

4 Preheat the oven to 180°C. Peel the onions and cut them into thin rings. Melt the butter in a roasting pan (c. 18 x 30 cm) on top of the stove. Add the onions and fry over medium heat for 6 minutes. Stir in the tomato purée, fry for 2 minutes, dust with the flour and fry for another 1 minute. Pour in the meat stock, stir in the caraway seeds, bring to the boil and place the cabbage rolls into the pan. Bake in the oven (centre, convection 160°C) for 1 hour 30 minutes until soft, turning the cabbage rolls once or twice during the cooking time.

5 About 5 minutes before the end of cooking time, place the bacon in a cold frying pan, add the oil. Heat the pan and fry the bacon for 3–4 minutes until crisp, turning it occasionally. Take the bacon out of the pan, leave to drain on kitchen paper.

6 Take the pan out of the oven. Remove the kitchen twine from the cabbage rolls, then arrange on a platter or individual plates, add the bacon. Transfer the meat stock into a tall jug, add the butter and briefly mix with a handheld mixer. Season with salt and pepper, serve with the cabbage rolls. Best enjoyed with potato purée (p.95) or boiled potatoes.

What was normal and everyday in the past is today celebrated as a culinary feast. Slaughter in the farmyard is now a rare thing – but the desire for freshly slaughtered meat (a Schlachtplatte) is still as great as ever. Why not ask your butcher when they have their slaughter and sausage-making days? This way you'll be able to buy the best black puddings and liver sausages.

FRIED SAUSAGE WITH PRETZEL CRUMBS

HEARTY AND SUBSTANTIAL

SERVES 4:

2 stale pretzels
2 tbsp flour | 2 eggs (medium)
salt | freshly ground black pepper
8 slices sausage with spleen (weighing c. 85 g each and 1 cm thick)
4 tsp medium-hot mustard (plus a little more for serving)
4 tbsp clarified butter

HOW LONG IT TAKES: c. 20 Min.
PER SERVING: c. 700 kcal | 37 g p | 52 g f | 16 g ch

1 Cut the pretzels into large pieces, then finely crush in a blender and transfer to a bowl. Put the flour into a deep plate, beat the eggs in another deep plate and season with salt and pepper. Spread the sausage slices on both sides with mustard. Turn them first in the flour, then in the beaten eggs and finally coat them with the pretzel crumbs.

2 In a large frying pan, melt 2 tablespoons of clarified butter. Add half the sausage slices and fry over medium heat for 2 minutes until golden, then turn and fry the other side over low heat for another 2 minutes. Lift the sausage slices out of the pan, drain on kitchen paper (keep them warm in the oven at 120°C if necessary). Put the remaining butter into the pan, add the remaining sausage slices and fry until golden. Serve with extra mustard. A potato and cucumber salad makes a good side dish (p.45).

FRIED LIVERWURST AND BLACK PUDDING

AS BAVARIAN AS IT GETS

SERVES 2:

2 liverwursts | 2 black puddings (150 g each)
400 g boiled potatoes, in their skins (from the day before)
½ onion | 1 sprig marjoram
2 sprigs flat-leaved parsley | 1½ tbsp clarified butter
salt | 1 level tsp caraway seeds
freshly ground black pepper
medium-hot mustard to serve

HOW LONG IT TAKES: c. 20 min
PER SERVING: c. 1150 kcal | 43 g p | 96 g f | 28 g ch

1 Skin the sausages, cut into 1 cm thick slices. Peel the potatoes and cut into 1 cm thick slices. Peel the onion and cut into thin strips. Rinse and shake dry the herbs, pull off and roughly chop the leaves.

2 In a large frying pan, heat 1 tablespoon of clarified butter. Place the potato slices side by side in it and sauté over medium heat for 3 minutes until golden, turn, season with salt and caraway seeds. Add the onion and fry for another 4 minutes. Take the potatoes out of the pan and set aside.

3 Melt the remaining butter in the pan. Add the black pudding slices, fry briefly on both sides, add the liverwurst slices and warm through. Add in the potatoes and the herbs, season wth salt and pepper. Serve immediately on warm plates or straight from the frying pan with the mustard.

JUST AS TASTY

Place the whole sausages into lightly salted, boiling water and simmer for about 15 minutes. Serve with potato purée (p.95) and sauerkraut (p.202).

LET'S GO, IT'S SLAUGHTERING DAY!

Bavaria celebrates many holidays and feast days where special dishes are served. One of the region's most important non-religious days was that on which the animals, which had been fattened up throughout the year, faced their destiny. In late autumn, the butcher would come to the farm to slaughter the animals in the presence of the entire family and staff – a bloody but all the more meaningful event for many farming families.

In doing so, the butcher's full artistry would be on display. Once the animal had bled dry, he would dismember it on the spot while still warm. He would then spend the next two hours efficiently processing every part of the animal – the meat and the offal – in the sausage kitchen. Every move had to be just right. And so it was that specialities like Brühwurst (boiled sausage), Zungenwurst (blood tongue sausage), Presssack (brawn or head cheese), fresh Blutwurst (blood sausage), fresh Leberwurst (liver sausage) and Griebenschmalz (crackling lard) were born. Boiled ham was made by pickling and smoking the meat. Sausages were smoked as a means of preservation. The exact recipes for each sausage and ham, however, remained the farmer's wife's or butcher's carefully guarded secret. Only God knows what they contain.

Once the arduous day's work was done, the farmers would hold a large "slaughter feast", where people of all ages would sit together, their plates full of cabbage, blood sausages, liver sausages, boiled pork belly and a rich meat soup, and give thanks to God for their plentiful food. This would be accompanied by a few Mass of beer to ensure the day ended on a cheerful note.

The abundant pickings from the slaughtering day meant the people could still enjoy hearty meals of meat, sausage and ham throughout the cold weeks and months which followed. But they did have to make sure their supplies were kept cool to prevent them from spoiling. As there was no technical equipment available for this during pre-industrial times, it was simply a question of relying on the predictable drop in outside temperatures from about October onwards, and placing the meat, preserved meats, smoked sausages and smoked ham in cold earthen cellars or larders.

This slaughtering day not only provided people with vital food; it was also an important milestone in farming life, for it signalled the end of the financial year. It was soon followed by St Martin's Day on 11 November, which finally brought the year of hard work to its conclusion. This was known as "main pay day", when farmhands and maidservants received their wages, new lease agreements were signed, and taxes were paid. It was also the time when workers could change employers.

As taxes used to be paid in kind, often a goose, the custom of eating the St Martin's goose on this day was established – and is still continued in many parts of Bavaria and beyond even today.

SOUR LIGHTS

Cooked lungs are not everyone's choice especially as they are not great to look at. Choose veal lights, which are tender and have a delicate taste. Here they are prepared to a traditional Bavarian recipe with a dark roux and then finished off with vinegar.

HEARTY AND AUTHENTICALLY BAVARIAN

SERVES 4–6:

80 g flour
6 tbsp vegetable oil
1 l beef broth (p.52, or ready-made beef stock)
3 large onions
2 bay leaves
4 cloves
1 kg marinated calf's lights (cut into ½ cm wide and 6 cm long strips, pre-order from the butcher)
80 g butter
2 sprigs flat-leaved parsley
salt | freshly ground black pepper
2 pinches of sugar
1–2 tbsp white or white wine vinegar (according to taste)

HOW LONG IT TAKES: c. 1 hour
PER SERVING (when serving 6):
c. 485 kcal | 39 g p | 28 g f | 12 g ch

1 In a wide saucepan, stir together the flour and the oil and heat gently. Fry for 7–8 minutes, stirring constantly, until the flour is dark brown. Add 1 ladle of beef broth and stir until smooth, then add the remaining broth, a little at a time, slowly bring to the boil and simmer for about 5 minutes. Peel the onions, halve 1 onion and push the bay leaves and the cloves into the onion halves.

2 Briefly rinse the strips of calf's lights, drain well and place into the saucepan, add the studded onion halves. Bring everything to the boil, then simmer for about 30 minutes over low heat, stirring frequently.

3 Finely dice the remaining onions. Melt the butter in a frying pan, add the onion dice and fry over medium heat for about 10 minutes until golden. Rinse and shake dry the parsley, pull off and finely chop the leaves and add them to the onions at the end. Season with a little salt and pepper.

4 Season the finished lights with salt, pepper and sugar, then flavour to taste with the vinegar. Arrange and serve on warm plates with the fried onions. Good with bread dumplings (p.89), boiled potatoes or bread rolls.

SOUR CALVES' LIVER

Calves' liver is probably the most popular of the offal. They are tender, only have a faint liver taste and are as soft as butter if cooked correctly.

QUICKLY MADE AND SOFT AS BUTTER

SERVES 4:

1 large onion
4 slices calves' liver (c. 800 g, cleaned, see tip)
1 tbsp flour
2 tbsp clarified butter
salt
2 tbsp cider vinegar
2 tbsp nutritional yeast flakes (from the organic store)
400 ml meat stock (from the jar)
1 tsp coarse-grained mustard
1 tsp medium-hot mustard
freshly ground black pepper
2–3 pinches of sugar

HOW LONG IT TAKES: c. 20 min
PER SERVING:
c. 360 kcal | 42 g p | 15 g f | 15 g ch

1 Peel and quarter the onion, then cut it diagonally into thin strips. Cut the liver into wide strips and dust evenly with the flour. Melt 1 tablespoon of clarified butter in a large frying pan. Add the liver and fry over medium heat for 2 minutes. Season lightly with salt, add 1 tablespoon of vinegar, cook for another 1 minute and place on a preheated plate.

2 Melt the remaining butter in the pan, add the onion and fry for about 3 minutes until golden. Stir in the yeast flakes, add the meat stock and cook for 2 minutes. Stir in the remaining vinegar and cook the sauce for another 2 minutes. Stir in the two types of mustard, simmer gently for another 1 minute.

3 Add the liver to the pan and stir to combine with the sauce. Take the pan off the heat and leave the liver to cook in the residual heat for about 3 minutes to be "pink". Season with salt, pepper and sugar. Serve the sour calves' liver with potato purée (p.95), boiled potatoes or bread rolls.

USEFUL TIP

Make sure the liver is free from membranes, sinews and veins (best ask the butcher to clean it). If the outer membrane is still attached, for example, the liver will contract when fried.

BREADED PORK CHOPS IN EGG SAUCE

A really good pork chop can be recognized by its thick, white layer of fat. It's only the fat which keeps the otherwise lean meat nice and juicy when fried.

AROMATIC AND JUICY

SERVES 4:

For the sauce:

3 eggs (medium) | 100 g low-fat sour cream
100 g sour cream
salt | freshly ground black pepper
a pinch of sugar | ½ bunch chives

For the chops:

5 slices dry toast
2 eggs (medium) | 2 tbsp cream
salt | freshly ground black pepper
2 pinches of ground caraway seeds
a few dashes of lemon juice
2 tbsp flour
4 pork chops (c. 250 g each, with a thick, fatty edge)
8 tbsp clarified butter
1 tbsp butter
lemon wedges to serve
Plus: meat tenderizer

HOW LONG IT TAKES: c. 40 min
PER SERVING: c. 695 kcal | 52 g p | 44 g f | 12 g ch

1 To make the sauce, place the eggs into a saucepan with boiling water and cook for 10 minutes until hard, then drain and cool under cold water. Shell and halve the eggs, then remove the egg yolks and put them into a small bowl. Using a whisk, stir the egg yolks until you have a smooth mixture, then add the two types of sour cream and stir in. Season with salt, pepper and sugar. Finely chop the egg whites. Rinse and drain the chives, then snip them into thin rings. Stir both into the sauce.

2 To cook the chops, cut the crusts off the toast, put the toast into a blender and process to fine breadcrumbs; transfer the crumbs to a bowl. Put the eggs into a deep plate and whisk with the cream, then season with salt, pepper, caraway seeds and lemon juice. Put the flour into another deep plate.

3 Flatten the pork chops a little by pounding them on both sides with the flat side of a meat tenderizer. Season the chops with salt and pepper, then turn them first in the flour, then in the eggs and finally coat them with the breadcrumbs.

4 Melt the clarified butter in two large frying pans. Add the pork chops and fry over medium heat for about 2 minutes, turn and fry for another 2 minutes, moistening them with the juices. Turn the chops again and fry over low heat for another 4 minutes. Put the butter in pats on top of the chops, season with a little salt to taste. Leave the butter to melt for 2 minutes and finish frying the chops.

5 Take the pork chops out of the pan, pat dry briefly with kitchen paper. Arrange the chops on preheated plates with the egg sauce and the lemon wedges. Tastes great served with a simple potato salad (p.45).

USEFUL TIP

By the way: the crisp breaded pork chops are equally delicious eaten cold as a Brotzeit dish.

CRISPY PORK ROAST WITH MEAT STOCK

An authentic Bavarian pork roast has to be tender and juicy, with a crispy rind that crackles and crunches when you take a bite. Our recipe has it all, and even something to nibble off the bone. The roast tastes best fresh from the oven – reheating doesn't work at all.

INCREDIBLY HEARTY

SERVES 4:

2 garlic cloves
1 heaped tsp caraway seeds | salt
800 g pork belly | 800 g pork neck
400 g spare ribs (cut apart between the ribs)
400 g pork tails (chopped, if liked, pre-order from the butcher)
1 small carrot | 400 g onions
1 tbsp vegetable oil | freshly ground black pepper
Plus: aluminium foil

HOW LONG IT TAKES: c. 30 min
IN THE OVEN: c. 3 hours
PER SERVING: c. 1065 kcal | 77 g p | 84 g f | 0 g ch

1 Peel the garlic, chop as finely as possible together with the caraway seeds and 1 heaped teaspoon salt. Rub the spiced salt mix over the pork neck and the meat side of the pork belly. Briefly wash the spare ribs and the pork tails, in order to remove bone or cartilage splinters, then pat dry. Peel and finely chop the carrot and the onions.

2 Heat the oil in a deep roasting pan (c. 25 x 35 cm) on top of the stove. Add the spare ribs and pork tails and fry over high heat for 2 minutes, turn them over, then fry for another 1 minute. Add the onions and fry for 1 minute, add the carrot and fry everything together for about 5 minutes, stirring constantly. Pour in 200 ml water, scraping up the frying juices with a spoon, then cook to reduce. Pour in 800 ml water and bring to the boil.

3 Place the pork neck and the pork belly with the rind side down into the pan. Cook in the oven (centre, best in a convection oven at 150°C, or preheated to 170°C top and bottom heat) for about 1 hour. Turn the meat pieces and the ribs. Using a sharp knife, cut into the pork belly rind at about 1-cm intervals so that it will be easy later on to slice the meat. Roast everything for another 1 hour 50 minutes, until the meat is cooked. Turn the meat pieces several times during the roasting time, and add a further 400 ml water, a little at a time.

4 Set the oven to the grill function (at the highest level). Take the pan out of the oven, remove the pork belly and wrap it with aluminium foil so that only the meat side is covered, while the pork rind is open and visible on top. Place the pork belly onto a rack, return it to the oven and grill for 5–10 minutes until crispy. In the meantime, place the roasting pan on top of the stove, take out the pork tails if using. Bring everything to the boil, scraping the meat juices off the sides of the roaster. Season the sauce to taste with salt and pepper.

5 Cut up the pork belly and the pork neck and arrange on plates, pour over the meat stock. Potato or bread dumplings (pp.86/87) and Bavarian cabbage salad (p.199) make good side dishes.

USEFUL TIP

The pork tails give the meat stock its typical consistency – but you don't have to use them; roasting the ribs gives your dish its wonderful colour.

PORK KNUCKLE AS IT OUGHT TO BE

Together with the pork roast, the pork knuckle is probably one of the most popular and best-known hearty dishes hailing from Bavaria. The strong, marbled muscle flesh of a pig's back legs makes the roast knuckles particularly juicy.

A BAVARIAN ORIGINAL

SERVES 4:

1 large garlic clove
1 tsp caraway seeds
salt
2 large pork knuckles (c. 1.4 kg each)
300 g onions
1 piece celeriac (c. 130 g)
1 carrot
400 ml meat stock (from the jar)
1 tsp cornflour
freshly ground black pepper
Plus: aluminium foil

HOW LONG IT TAKES: c. 30 min
IN THE OVEN: c. 3 hours 50 min
PER SERVING: c. 880 kcal | 87 g p | 56 g f | 7 g ch

1 Preheat the oven to 160°C. Peel the garlic, cut into thin slices, sprinkle with ½ tsp caraway seeds and 1 tablespoon of salt, then chop very finely. Rub the pork knuckles on the meaty sides only and under the rinds with the spiced salt. Sprinkle the rind with salt and massage firmly into the rind.

2 Peel the onions, celeriac and carrot and chop into 1 cm cubes. Spread the vegetables in a deep roasting pan (c. 25 x 35 cm), place the pork knuckles on top. Put the roaster into the oven (centre, convection 140°C) and roast for 1 hour 15 minutes. Turn the knuckles over, roast for another 15 minutes. Pour in the meat stock and roast for 1 hour 30 minutes to 2 hours until tender (see tips), turning every 30 minutes.

3 Take the pan out of the oven, wrap the bones of the knuckles in aluminium foil. Stir ½ teaspoon of salt into a good dash of water and brush the rinds with a little of the salted water.

4 Increase the oven temperature to 250°C (convection 230°C) . Place the pork knuckles onto a rack, put back into the oven (centre), and place a baking tray with water as a dripping guard underneath. Roast the knuckles for about 20 minutes until crisp, turning and brushing the rinds regularly with salt water. They should be nicely browned all over and have a crust.

5 Meanwhile, generously skim the fat off the vegetables and the stock (see tips). Put the pan on top of the stove, bring the stock to the boil. Stir the cornflour into 1–2 tbsp cold water until smooth, then stir into the stock, simmer for 3 minutes until you have a velvety sauce. Season with salt, pepper and the remaining caraway seeds.

6 Take the crisp pork knuckles out of the oven. Using a sharp knife, halve each one along the bones and serve with the sauce on preheated plates. Good with potato dumplings (p.88), red cabbage or Bavarian cabbage salad (pp.200/201).

USEFUL TIPS

The cooking time for pork knuckles may vary, so you should check after 3 hours by pushing a fork into the meat as to whether they are done.
Season the skimmed-off fat with salt and pepper, leave to cool and enjoy as dripping on bread.

Bratwurst
Schweinswürstel
Fleischspieß
Wiener, Bockwurst

A TASTY, RICH MEAT STOCK

ABSOLUTELY FABULOUS WHEN HOMEMADE

MAKES C. 800 ML SAUCE:

1 kg meaty veal and pork bones (chopped into large chunks)
200 g onions | 1 carrot
1 piece celeriac (c. 200 g)
2 tbsp vegetable oil | 2 tbsp tomato purée
½ l full-bodied red wine (e.g. Cabernet Sauvignon)
1 tbsp flour | 100 ml sherry (medium dry)
1.6 l veal stock (from a jar)
2 tbsp marinated pot roast seasoning (see tips, p.176)
2 sage leaves | a pinch of sugar
salt | freshly ground black pepper

HOW LONG IT TAKES: c. 45 min
IN THE SAUCEPAN: c. 3 hours 15 min
PER SERVING: c. 1045 kcal | 209 g p | 43 g f | 69 g ch

1 Preheat the oven to 220°C. Arrange the bones on a baking tray and cook in the oven (centre, convection 200°C) for about 30 minutes until browned all over.

2 Peel and finely chop onions, carrot and celeriac. Heat the oil in a wide saucepan, add the onions and fry over medium heat for about 3 minutes. Add the carrot and the celeriac, fry for another 5 minutes. Take the bones out of the oven and add them to the vegetables, stir in the tomato purée and fry everything for another 5 minutes, stirring constantly.

3 Pour a dash of red wine over the bones and vegetables, simmer to reduce. Dust with the flour, add more wine and reduce. Add the remaining wine and the sherry, cook to reduce. Pour in the veal stock and bring to the boil. Leave the sauce to simmer gently over low heat for 1 hour, add the pot roast seasoning and simmer for another 2 hours.

4 Strain the sauce in a fine sieve, catching the sauce in a small saucepan. Add the sage and bring to the boil, simmer for about 15 minutes to reduce until creamy, then remove the sage. Season the sauce with sugar, salt and pepper.

FRIED BEEF WITH ONIONS

In beef cuts for quick-frying, like the sirloin used here, the quality and the degree of maturity of the meat are of major importance for success. The beef loin should be evenly marbled and have a delicate fatty edge.

TASTES BEST AT HOME

SERVES 4:
1 kg deep-frying fat
1½ large onions
1½ tbsp flour
1 level tsp sweet paprika
1 garlic clove
2 sprigs thyme
4 marbled sirloin steaks
(c. 220 g each, with a fatty edge)
salt
2 tbsp vegetable oil
1 tbsp butter
400 ml meat stock (homemade, p.76, or ready-made stock to stir in)
freshly ground black pepper
Plus: meat tenderizer | baking paper

HOW LONG IT TAKES: c. 30 min
PER SERVING: c. 560 kcal | 76 g p | 29 g f | 14 g ch

1 Preheat the oven to 120°C (convection 100°C), line a baking tray with baking paper and put it into the oven (centre). Heat the deep-frying fat in a tall saucepan (to 160–170°C). The fat will have reached the correct temperature when you hold a wooden spoon into the fat and small bubbles immediately begin to form.

2 Meanwhile, peel the onions and cut or shave them as thinly as possible into rings. Put the onion rings into a large bowl, dust with the flour and the paprika and stir well to combine.

3 Put about one-third of the onions into the hot fat, separate carefully with a cooking spoon or a meat fork and deep-fry for about 2 minutes until golden. Lift out with a slotted spoon, drain briefly on kitchen paper, then put on the lined tray in the oven to keep them warm. Deep-fry the remaining onions and also keep them warm in the oven.

4 Don't peel the garlic, only press it lightly to flatten with the back of a knife. Rinse and shake dry the thyme. Flatten the beef loin slices slightly on both sides by pounding them with the flat side of a meat tenderizer. Season with salt.

5 Heat the oil in a large frying pan. Add the meat slices and fry over medium heat for about 2 minutes, then add the garlic and the thyme. Turn the meat and fry for another 2 minutes – also fry the fatty edges; to do so, lean the slices against the frying pan sides. Add the butter to the frying pan, turn the meat in the butter all over, take the pan off the stove and leave the meat in the pan to cook in the residual heat for 6 minutes until "pink".

6 Bring the meat stock to the boil. Grind pepper over the beef loin slices, then serve with the meat stock and the roasted onion rings. Best enjoyed with sautéed or creamy potatoes (p.94).

USEFUL TIP

These sirloin steaks also taste delicious with herb butter instead of the meat stock. As an accompaniment, serve with a freshly dressed green salad.

BEEF GOULASH

Beef shanks are particularly well-suited to making a goulash. The muscular meat is nicely marbled, with plenty of sinews and fat, ensuring that the meat stays juicy during cooking. If you find shanks too streaky, use a piece from the shoulder instead.

IRRESISTIBLE AND JUICY

SERVES 4:

450 g onions
1 kg beef shanks (without bones)
salt | freshly ground black pepper
1 tsp hot paprika
3 tsp sweet paprika
1 tbsp flour | 4 tbsp vegetable oil
2 tbsp tomato purée
200 ml red wine (e.g. Cabernet Sauvignon)
800 ml meat stock (from a jar)
½ garlic clove
finely grated zest of ½ organic lemon

HOW LONG IT TAKES: c. 45 min
IN THE SAUCEPAN: c. 1 hour 45 min
PER SERVING: c. 575 kcal | 57 g p | 30 g f | 11 g ch

1 Peel the onions and cut them into ½ cm cubes. Cut the beef shanks into about 2 cm cubes, then put them into a bowl. Dust with salt, pepper, paprika and flour. With your hands, turn the meat cubes in the bowl so that the flour and the spices coat them well.

2 In a large wide saucepan, heat 3 tablespoons of oil. Add half the meat and fry over medium heat for 3 minutes, turning, until browned all over; take out. Heat the remaining oil in the saucepan and fry the remaining meat for about 3 minutes and remove. Add the onions and fry for 2 minutes. Return the fried meat cubes to the saucepan and cook everything for another 3 minutes.

3 Stir the tomato purée into the meat and onion mixture and cook for 5 minutes, stirring constantly, scraping and loosening any sediment stuck to the base of the pan with a wooden spoon. Pour in the wine and leave to reduce for 3 minutes, then pour in the meat stock and bring to the boil. Cover the beef goulash and simmer over low heat for about 1 hour 45 minutes until tender and cooked.

4 Peel and very finely chop the garlic, then combine with the lemon zest. Season the finished goulash with salt and pepper, stir in the lemon and garlic mixture and bring to the boil again. Arrange on warm plates and serve with pasta, rice, potatoes, potato dumplings or bread dumplings (pp.88/89).

USEFUL TIP

Beef goulash can easily be prepared in larger quantities. Simply leave everything that is not eaten to cool completely, spoon into freezer boxes or bags and put it into the freezer. Alternatively, bring the remaining goulash to the boil, then spoon it into thoroughly cleaned screw-top jars. Close the jars tightly, place them upside down on a kitchen towel and leave to cool. The preserved goulash will keep for several weeks in the fridge. If you do not wish to wait that long, simply reheat the goulash the following day – after reheating, the goulash will taste even better than when first prepared.

GULASCH

BEEF ROULADES WITH GHERKINS AND BACON

A genuine classic – beloved by everyone, across the generations!

WORTH THE EFFORT

SERVES 4:

For the beef roulades:

1 carrot | salt
2 onions
4 slices of brisket or rump steak (c. 200 g each, pounded thin)
freshly ground black pepper
4 tsp medium-hot mustard
12 rashers bacon (c. 120 g)
4 gherkin sticks (or 1 large gherkin, quartered lengthways)
2 good pinches of flour

For the sauce:

1 large onion | 1 carrot
1 piece celeriac (c. 80 g)
3 tbsp vegetable oil
1 tbsp tomato purée
300 ml full-bodied red wine (e.g. Cabernet Sauvignon)
1 l meat stock (from the jar)
1 tsp cornflour
salt | freshly ground black pepper

Plus:

kitchen twine or cocktail sticks

HOW LONG IT TAKES: c. 1 hour
IN THE SAUCEPAN: c. 1 hour 40 min
PER SERVING: c. 680 kcal | 49 g p | 44 g f | 12 g ch

1 To make the roulades, peel the carrot, halve it crossways, then quarter the halves lengthways. Put the carrot strips (about 1 cm wide) into boiling salted water, cook for 2 minutes, remove, rinse under cold water and drain. Peel the onions, cut into 8 wedges.

2 Place the steaks on the work surface, season with salt and pepper and spread with mustard. On each steak, place 3 bacon rashers lengthways, and put 2 carrot sticks, 2 onion wedges and 1 gherkin stick into the lower third. Fold over the long sides of the steaks, then roll up from the short ends. Fasten with kitchen twine or cocktail sticks.

3 Season the roulades with salt and pepper, dust all over with flour and place into the saucepan. Fry in the oil over medium heat for 3 minutes, turn and fry for another 3 minutes. Take the roulades out of the saucepan.

4 To make the sauce, peel the onion, carrot and celeriac and cut into 1 cm cubes. Heat the oil in a large, wide saucepan. Put the cubes into the saucepan and fry for 2 minutes. Stir in the tomato purée and fry for a further 3 minutes. Add a dash of red wine and cook to reduce, repeat twice. Now pour in the remaining red wine and the meat stock, bring to the boil. Place the roulades in the sauce, cover and cook over low heat for 1 hour 40 minutes or until tender.

5 Take the roulades out of the saucepan. Strain the sauce through a sieve, catching the sauce and returning it to the saucepan, bring to the boil. Dissolve the cornflour in 1–2 tablespoons cold water and stir into the sauce, cook over medium heat for 15 minutes to reduce until it has a velvety consistency. Season with salt and pepper. Return the roulades to the saucepan, bring to the boil and gently simmer in the sauce over low heat for another 2–3 minutes to warm through. Serve on warm plates with potato purée (p.95) or wide ribbon noodles.

BEEF BRISKET WITH PUMPKIN AND TURNIPS

You can use various cuts for braising: brisket, short ribs, flank and slices of rump are all marbled, streaky and make a really strong and very flavoursome broth, the sort that every good kitchen should have. If however you prefer it a little more delicate, just go for topside.

DOWN TO EARTH AND AUTUMNAL

SERVES 4:

400 g butternut squash
600 g waxy potatoes
250 g turnips | 1 large onion
2 tbsp butter | salt
freshly cooked beef brisket plus
½ l beef broth (both p.52)
1 bay leaf
4 sprigs flat-leaved parsley
1 small bunch chives
1 piece horseradish (c. 10 cm)
freshly ground black pepper
freshly grated nutmeg

HOW LONG IT TAKES: c. 50 min (plus the preparation time for the beef brisket)
PER SERVING: c. 790 kcal | 65 g p | 45 g f | 26 g ch

1 Peel the pumpkin and remove the seeds as well as all the fibrous flesh. Peel the potatoes and the turnips. Cut everything into 1½ cm cubes. Peel and finely dice the onion.

2 Melt the butter in a large, wide saucepan. Add the onion and sauté over medium heat for 3 minutes until translucent. Add the turnips and the potatoes, add a little salt and fry for 5 minutes. Pour over the beef broth and bring to the boil.

3 Add the pumpkin and the bay leaf to the saucepan, cover and simmer the vegetables over low heat for about 10 minutes. Remove the lid and cook everything open for another 10 minutes until soft. Rinse and shake dry the herbs. Pull the leaves off the parsley sprigs and chop roughly, snip the chives into thin rings. Peel the horseradish.

4 Season the vegetables with salt, pepper and nutmeg, then sprinkle with the parsley. Cut the prepared, still-hot brisket into finger-sized slices and arrange these with the vegetables on warm plates. Pour over the sauce, sprinkle with the chives and serve. Put the horseradish on the table with a grater so that everyone can help themselves (see tips).

USEFUL TIPS

Meat is always cut against the grain of the fibres so that it will be meltingly tender on the tongue. If the meat is cut along the fibre, however, it will be tough. The turnips give a fine piquancy to the vegetables. To make it even spicier grate the fresh horseradish over the brisket and the vegetables, according to taste.

41423

GRAIN-FED ROAST CHICKEN

Quality is the be-all and end-all for success in a roast chicken, and differences can often only be made out after cooking. A good chicken will keep its shape when roasted, the flesh is juicy, and the crisp skin stays firmly attached to the meat.

DIVE STRAIGHT IN

SERVES 2:
2 tbsp butter
2 tbsp vegetable oil
1 level tsp hot paprika
1 level tsp sweet paprika
1 level tsp shish kebab spice (ready-mix)
salt | freshly ground black pepper
6 sprigs flat-leaved parsley
2 sprigs lovage (optional)
½ organic lemon
1 small onion
1 roasting chicken (c. 1.1 kg)
Plus: cocktail sticks

HOW LONG IT TAKES: c. 10 min
IN THE OVEN: c. 1 hour 30 min
PER SERVING: c. 870 kcal | 82 g p | 58 g f | 3 g ch

1 Preheat the oven to 150°C. Melt the butter in a frying pan. Stir in the oil, paprika and shish kebab spice mix, season with salt and pepper. Take off the stove. Rinse and shake dry the herbs, wash the half lemon under hot water, then quarter it. Peel and roughly dice the onion.

2 Pat the chicken dry inside and out with kitchen paper. If preferred, remove the parson's nose and the wing tips from the chicken. Generously season the inside of the chicken with salt and pepper. Fold over the herb stems and push them into the cavity together with the lemon and the onion. Close the opening well with cocktail sticks.

3 Thoroughly brush the chicken all over with the prepared paprika butter, reserving some of the butter for later. Place the chicken into a roasting pan, placing it on its side (see tip), and pour in 200 ml hot water. Put the pan into the oven (centre, convection 130°C), and cook the chicken for 30 minutes. Turn the chicken onto the other side, brush with more paprika butter and roast for another 45 minutes until the flesh is tender. Brush occasionally with the butter during cooking. At the end of the cooking time, push a wooden toothpick into the flesh between breast and leg; if the juices run clear the chicken is done. If not, leave to cook for a little longer.

4 Take the cooked chicken out of the oven, and set the oven to the grill function (highest level). Halve the chicken lengthways (using a large knife or a pair of poultry scissors), then cut out the backbone and discard the stuffing. Place the chicken halves onto the rack and return to the oven (centre), putting the roasting pan underneath as a drip guard. Grill the chicken for 10–15 minutes until golden brown and crisp, brushing it frequently with the remaining paprika butter.

5 Arrange the roast chicken on warm plates, drizzle with a little of the cooking juices and serve. Goes well with a potato salad (pp.44/45).

USEFUL TIP

When roasting a chicken, place it on the leg sides. This way, part of the breast is always covered with liquid and will therefore stay nice and moist.

POTATO DUMPLINGS

Choosing the right type of potato is of great importance – it's the only way to ensure the dumplings stick together and have plenty of flavour. Best suited are floury potatoes, such as King Edward and Maris Pipers.

LOVELY AND FLUFFY

SERVES 4
(makes about 8 dumplings):

For the dumplings:
2.5 kg floury potatoes (e.g. Desiree or Maris Piper)
salt
½ pack dumpling aid (c. 2.5 g; prevents the dumplings from turning brown)

For the crumbed butter:
1 slice dry toast
2 tbsp butter

Plus:
potato ricer
potato grater

HOW LONG IT TAKES: c. 50 min
IN THE SAUCEPAN: c. 30 min
PER SERVING:
c. 390 kcal | 10 g p | 5 g f | 76 g ch

1 To make the dumplings, wash the potatoes. Cook 500 g in salted water for 20–25 minutes until done. Drain, then return to the stove, leave to steam over low heat for 5 minutes. Peel and leave to cool, then push through a potato ricer into a bowl.

2 Meanwhile, peel the remaining potatoes and finely grate them into a bowl. Sprinkle the gratings with dumpling aid, combine well and leave to stand for about 10 minutes (starch will separate and settle in the bottom of the bowl in this time). Then put the potato mash into a cloth and firmly wring out.

3 Add the raw potatoes and the settled starch to the boiled potatoes. Generously season the mixture with salt, combine well and shape into 8 even-sized dumplings. Put into a saucepan with plenty of boiling salted water and bring back to the boil. As soon as all the dumplings float to the surface, put the lid onto the saucepan at an angle and leave the dumplings to simmer over low heat for about 30 minutes.

4 To make the crumb butter, finely grate the toast. Melt the butter in a small frying pan. Add the crumbs and fry for about 2 minutes until golden. Lift dumplings out of the water and drain. Arrange on plates, drizzle with the butter and serve.

BREAD DUMPLINGS

Bavaria can't do without bread dumplings, especially when there's a lovely sauce to be mopped up – with roast pork, roast beef, goulash or game.

DELICIOUSLY LIGHT

SERVES 4
(makes about 8 dumplings):

150 ml milk
300 g day-old bread rolls cut into slices or large cubes
1 large onion
4–6 sprigs flat-leaved parsley
2 tbsp butter
4 eggs (medium)
salt | freshly ground black pepper
freshly grated nutmeg
½ bunch chives

HOW LONG IT TAKES: c. 35 min
IN THE SAUCEPAN: c. 25 min
PER SERVING:
c. 325 kcal | 15 g p | 12 g f | 39 g ch

1 Heat the milk to lukewarm. Put the bread into a bowl and pour over the milk, leave to soak for 5 minutes. Peel and finely dice the onion. Rinse and shake dry, then roughly chop the parsley. Melt the butter in a frying pan, add the onion and fry for 3 minutes until translucent. Stir in the parsley.

2 Whisk the eggs and add with the onion mixture to the soaked bread. Season with salt, pepper and nutmeg, stir and leave to rest for 10 minutes. Divide the mixture into eight portions. With moistened hands shape into eight dumplings.

3 In a large saucepan, bring plenty of water to the boil, add salt. Put the dumplings into the water and cook for about 5 minutes, then cover and simmer gently over low heat for about 20 minutes. Rinse and shake dry the chives, snip into thin rings. Using a slotted spoon, lift the dumplings out of the water, into a bowl or plates and sprinkle with the chives.

USEFUL TIP

Depending on the bread you are using you will need to "juggle" with the milk quantities. If the bread is very dry, you may need another 50 ml milk. If the mixture is too moist, simply stir in 1–2 tablespoons of breadcrumbs.

SERVIETTE DUMPLINGS

In times gone by, serviette dumplings were wrapped in a cotton cloth, hence the name. Today we mostly use clingfilm or aluminium foil to wrap them.

UNBEATABLY GOOD

SERVES 4–6:

1 large onion
2 bread rolls (c. 130 g)
70 g butter
¼ l milk
250 g day-old bread rolls, cut into slices or large chunks
6 eggs (medium)
6 sprigs flat-leaved parsley
salt | freshly ground black pepper
freshly grated nutmeg
Plus: aluminium foil and clingfilm

HOW LONG IT TAKES: c. 35 min
IN THE SAUCEPAN: c. 40 min
PER SERVING (when serving 6):
c. 375 kcal | 14 g p | 18 g f | 39 g ch

1 Peel and finely dice the onion. Cut the rolls into 1 cm dice. In a large frying pan, melt 40 g butter. Add the bread rolls, fry for 3–4 minutes until golden, then take out. Melt the remaining butter in the pan, add the onion and fry for 2 minutes until translucent. Heat the milk to lukewarm.

2 Put the slices or chunks of to bread rolls into a bowl and cover with milk. Add the fried bread cubes, onion and eggs, leave to rest for 20 minutes (without combining!). Meanwhile, rinse and shake dry the parsley, pull off and chop the leaves.

3 Add the parsley to the dumpling mixture, season with salt, pepper and nutmeg, loosely combine everything. Spread out 2 large pieces of aluminium foil, cover with same-sized pieces of clingfilm. Spread half the dumpling mix lengthways on each set of foils, wrap the dumplings in rolls as large, waterproof “sticks of rock” (c. 25 cm long), with the ends twisted.

4 Bring plenty of water to the boil in a large wide saucepan. Place the dumplings into the water and leave to simmer for 20 minutes with the lid at an angle. Turn off the heat and leave the dumplings to cook for another 20 minutes in the hot water. Lift the dumplings out of the water, unwrap, slice and serve.

PRETZEL DUMPLINGS

Did you know that not all gugelhupfs are sweet? A simple savoury dumpling mixture makes for a feast for the eyes and the palate.

CLEVER GUGELHUPF DUMPLING

SERVES 4:

4 stale pretzels
(but not too hard)
150 ml milk
250 g onions
80 g butter
6 sprigs flat-leaved parsley
4 eggs (medium)
salt | freshly ground black pepper
freshly grated nutmeg
butter and breadcrumbs
for the dish

Plus:

gugelhupf cake mould (c. 1 l volume)

HOW LONG IT TAKES: c. 35 min
IN THE OVEN: c. 50 min
PER SERVING:
c. 425 kcal | 13 g p | 27 g f | 32 g ch

1 Cut the pretzels into 1 cm cubes and put into a bowl. Heat the milk to lukewarm and pour over the pretzels. Peel and finely dice the onions. Melt the butter in a frying pan, add the onions and fry for about 10 minutes until golden. Rinse and shake dry the parsley, finely chop the leaves and add to the onions at the end. Leave to cool.

2 Separate the eggs. Add the egg yolks and the onions to the pretzels, season with salt, pepper and nutmeg. Combine well and leave to swell for 10 minutes. Preheat the oven to 175°C. Beat the egg whites until stiff and fold into the pretzel mixture.

3 Grease the gugelhupf mould with butter, sprinkle with the breadcrumbs. Put the pretzel mixture into the mould, smooth the top and bang a few times onto the work surface so that any air bubbles disappear. Put the mould into a tall ovenproof saucepan or a tall roaster and add enough water to come three-quarters of the way up the sides of the mould.

Put the gugelhupf into the oven (centre, convection 155°C) and cook for 45–50 minutes. If it gets too dark on the surface, cover with aluminium foil. Take the mould out of the oven, tip out the gugelhupf, cut into thick slices and serve.

These classic side dishes are popular not only with children. They taste great with any kind of sauce – and of course they are excellent with braised dishes cooked in lots of meat stock.

SPAETZLE

SWABIAN SPECIALITY

SERVES 4:

300 g spaetzle flour or plain white flour
5 eggs (medium) | 4 egg yolks (medium)
salt | freshly grated nutmeg
3 tbsp butter
freshly ground black pepper
Plus: spaetzle maker or ricer

HOW LONG IT TAKES: c. 30 min
PER SERVING: c. 475 kcal | 19 g p | 20 g f | 54 g ch

1 Put the flour, eggs, egg yolks and 2 tablespoons of cold water into the bowl of a food processor (or work with a mixing bowl and a handheld mixer), season with salt and nutmeg. Using the kneading hooks, beat the mixture for about 10 minutes until you have a smooth, thick dough.

2 In a large, wide saucepan, bring plenty of salted water to the boil (see tip). Put a little of the dough into the spaetzle maker or ricer and press or shave the dough into the boiling water. Stir to separate with a cooking spoon, bring to the boil, briefly simmer. Lift out the spaetzle with a slotted spoon, transfer to a sieve, rinse under cold water and leave to drain. Make the remaining dough into spaetzle.

3 Melt the butter in a large frying pan until foaming. Add the spaetzle and warm through for 2–3 minutes. Season with salt, pepper and nutmeg.

USEFUL TIP

Make sure you fill the saucepan up to the rim with water! This allows the spaetzle to drop straight into the water and they stay a regular size as they have no time to lengthen in the air.

FINGER GNOCCHI

BAVARIAN-STYLE PASTA

SERVES 4:

1 day-old bread roll | 2 eggs (medium)
250 g flour | salt
freshly grated nutmeg
2–3 tbsp butter | freshly ground black pepper
flour for working

HOW LONG IT TAKES: c. 40 min
PER SERVING: c. 340 kcal | 11 g p | 9 g f | 53 g ch

1 Soak the roll in lukewarm water for 15 minutes, turning it several times, then squeeze out well and put into the bowl of a food processor (or work with a mixing bowl and a handheld mixer). Add the eggs and the flour to the bowl, season with salt and nutmeg. Using the kneading hooks, work all the ingredients for 3–4 minutes to form a smooth dough.

2 On a lightly floured work surface, roll out the dough to form 5 cm rolls, then cut into 1 cm slices and, with floured hands, shape into small sausages that are tapered at both ends. Bring plenty of salted water to the boil. Add the pasta in two portions and cook for 3 minutes each. Lift the cooked pasta out of the water with a slotted spoon, put into a sieve, rinse under cold water and leave to drain.

3 Melt the butter in a large frying pan. Add the pasta and fry for 1–2 minutes until just lightly golden (do not fry too dark or they will dry out). Season with salt and pepper to taste, then serve.

CREAMY POTATO GRATIN

EASY AND GOOD

SERVES 4:
1 kg waxy potatoes
2 tbsp butter
1 large onion
1 small garlic clove
100 g grated Emmental cheese
400 g cream
salt | freshly ground black pepper
freshly grated nutmeg
Plus: aluminium foil

HOW LONG IT TAKES: c. 25 min
IN THE OVEN: c. 1 hour
PER SERVING: c. 590 kcal | 14 g p | 44 g f | 34 g ch

1 Wash and peel the potatoes, then shave into about 2 mm slices using a box grater. Grease an ovenproof dish (c. 18 x 30 cm) with ½ tablespoon of butter, then place the potato slices inside, overlapping like roof tiles.

2 Preheat the oven to 200°C. Peel, then finely dice the onion and the garlic. Melt 1 tablespoon of butter in a frying pan. Add the onion and the garlic and sauté for 3 minutes until translucent. Spread over the potatoes together with the grated cheese.

3 Season the cream to taste with salt, pepper and nutmeg, then pour it evenly over the potato slices. Dot with pats of the remaining butter, cover with aluminium foil. Place the potatoes into the oven (centre, convection 180°C) and bake for about 1 hour until they are golden brown, removing the foil after 45 minutes. Remove the gratin potatoes from the oven and leave to rest for a moment, then serve in the roasting dish.

USEFUL TIP

Potato gratin goes particularly well with pan-fried game, roast saddle of lamb, veal, beef and pork. It is an ideal accompaniment particularly for those dishes where there is little meat stock.

POTATO PURÉE

There is nothing more comforting than a nice potato purée. It makes you feel as if you're back home with Mum putting it on the table, and of course it's great for mopping up all the delicious sauces.

VELVETY AND BUTTERY

SERVES 4:
1 kg floury potatoes
salt
100 ml milk
freshly grated nutmeg
100 g butter
Plus: potato ricer

HOW LONG IT TAKES: c. 20 min
IN THE SAUCEPAN: c. 25 min
PER SERVING: c. 340 kcal | 5 g p | 22 g f | 31 g ch

1 Wash and peel the potatoes, then cut them into halves or quarters depending on their size. Put into a saucepan with plenty of salted water, bring to the boil and cook for about 15–20 minutes until the potatoes are cooked. Drain the water, return the saucepan to the stove and leave the potatoes to steam for about 5 minutes over low heat.

2 Bring the milk to the boil and season with salt and nutmeg. Cut the butter into small cubes.

3 Press the cooked potatoes through a potato ricer into a bowl or a saucepan – for a very smooth purée do so twice. Then stir the milk and the butter cubes into the purée, a little at a time, using a wooden spoon (see tips). Check and adjust the seaoning, if necessary, and serve.

USEFUL TIPS

Allowing the potatoes to steam out as described ensures that they are dry and helps to bind the purée. You can, however, also cook the potatoes in their skins, peel while still hot and then continue making the purée.
Never use the whisks of a handheld or stick mixer to stir the potato purée. It would not be light and airy, but tough and slippery.
To keep the potato purée hot, simply immerse the bowl in a hot water bath, cover with foil and stir again just before serving
You can vary the basic recipe in many different ways: stir in finely chopped curly endive lettuce, roasted onions, freshly chopped parsley or crisply fried bacon, for example.

OR TRY THIS: POTATO AND CELERIAC PURÉE

Wash and peel 600 g celeriac and 400 g floury potatoes, then cut into 1 cm cubes. Put them into a saucepan, pour in 200 g cream and 300 ml milk, season with salt, bring to the boil, cover and cook for about 25–30 minutes until soft. Boil the liquid to reduce until creamy. Press the celeriac and the potatoes through a potato ricer, add the remaining cooking liquid. Cut 80 g cold butter into small cubes and stir into the purée, a little at a time. Season with salt, freshly ground black pepper and freshly grated nutmeg. This purée makes a particularly delicious accompaniment to game dishes.

Many Bavarian dishes are accompanied by a mixed salad. Among the most popular types are cucumber, cabbage, radish and beetroot salds plus the ubiquitous green salad. All salads are very simply dressed, so that the taste of the main ingredient is not swamped by the dressing ingredients.

CUCUMBER SALAD

SIMPLY REFRESHING

SERVES 4:

1 large cucumber
salt
150 g sour cream
50 g natural yoghurt
2 tbsp white wine vinegar
1 tsp sugar
3 sprigs dill
freshly ground black pepper

HOW LONG IT TAKES: c. 10 min
STANDING: c. 20 min
PER SERVING: c. 70 kcal | 2 g p | 4 g f | 5 g ch

1 Wash the cucumber, then peel so that some strips of green peel remain. Grate or cut the cucumber into 2–3 mm slices. Put the slices into a bowl, add a little salt, leave to stand for 10 minutes.

2 Stir together the cream, yoghurt, vinegar and sugar. Rinse and shake dry the dill, pull off and finely chop the tips. Stir into the dressing.

3 Drain the watery cucumber liquid and lightly squeeze the cucumber slices, then stir in the sour cream dressing and leave to stand so that the flavours develop for about 10 minutes. Season the salad to taste with salt and pepper and serve.

CABBAGE SALAD

CRUNCHY AND PIQUANT

SERVES 4:

500 g young pointed cabbage | 1 large onion
4 tbsp vegetable oil | 1 tsp sugar
4 tbsp cider vinegar | 150 ml vegetable stock
salt | freshly ground black pepper
2 pinches of caraway seeds (whole or ground)

HOW LONG IT TAKES: c. 25 min
PER SERVING: c. 125 kcal | 2 g p | 10 g f | 5 g ch

1 Wash the cabbage and halve it lengthways, then cut it into thin strips, discarding the core. Put the cabbage into a bowl. Peel and finely dice the onion.

2 In a saucepan, heat 2 tablespoons of oil, fry the onion for 2–3 minutes until translucent. Add the sugar, cook for 1 minute to caramelize. Add vinegar and stock, season with salt, pepper and caraway.

3 Pour the hot marinade over the cabbage, combine well and check and adjust the seasoning with salt and pepper. Finally, stir in the remaining oil. Leave the salad to marinate for a while or serve right away and enjoy lukewarm.

USEFUL TIP

The hot marinade blanches the cabbage but it still stays crunchy. Young cababages are particularly well suited for this type of preparation. If you would like to use older cabbage, you should salt the cabbage strips and knead them thoroughly, before leaving the cabbage to stand for an extra 30 minutes. The liquid is then drained off, the cabbage squeezed out and only then should you continue as described here. Alternatively, briefly blanch the cabbage strips in boiling salted water, drain, rinse under ice-cold water and finally combine with the marinade and the remaining oil as above.

O MARIA
Trösterin der Betrübten
Bitt für uns

FRIDAY FOOD

Bavarians are Catholic, so Fridays – their day of penance – are meat-free. But that doesn't bother them at all, because they are just as fond of fish dishes or of course their beloved yeast dumplings.

EXTRA-BUTTERY BREAD SOUP WITH ONIONS IN BUTTER

Magicking an amazing meal out of very few ingredients, that's truly the art of cooking – an art that's mastered by Bavarian housewives.

EASY AND GOOD

SERVES 4:

250 g dark rye or spelt farmhouse bread (see tip)
1 large onion | 4 tbsp butter
1 l beef broth (p.52, or ready-made beef stock)
salt | freshly ground black pepper
freshly grated nutmeg (optional)
2 sprigs flat-leaved parsley

HOW LONG IT TAKES: c. 25 min
PER SERVING: c. 350 kcal | 17 g p | 15 g f | 28 g ch

1 Cut the bread into in 1½ cm cubes. Peel and halve the onion, then cut it into thin strips. Melt 2 tablespoons of butter in a large frying pan. Add the bread dice and fry over medium heat for 6–7 minutes until golden brown and crisp. Lift the fried bread out of the pan and leave to drain on kitchen paper. Melt the remaining butter in the pan, add the onion and fry over medium to high heat for about 10 minutes until golden brown.

2 Bring the beef broth to the boil, then season to taste with salt, pepper and a little nutmeg, if liked. Rinse and shake dry the parsley, pull off and finely chop the leaves.

3 Divide the bread cubes between warm plates, then pour over the beef broth. Sprinkle with the onion and the parsley and serve immediately.

EXTRA GOOD: HOME-BAKED SPELT BREAD

Put 600 g whole spelt flour and 150 g white spelt flour into the bowl of a food processor together with 1 heaped tablespoon of salt. Make a hollow in the centre and crumble in ½ cube fresh yeast (c. 20 g). Add 50 ml lukewarm water and stir to combine. Sprinkle in 1 heaped tablespoon of brown sugar, add 150 g sourdough starter (ready-made). Cover the bowl with a kitchen towel and leave the mixture to rise in a warm place for about 15 minutes. Now add to the bowl 450 ml lukewarm water, 1 level teaspoon each of ground coriander and caraway seeds and with the kneading hooks work everything to a smooth dough (this will take about 5–8 minutes). Knead the dough again with your hands on a lightly floured work surface, then shape it into a longish loaf. Place the loaf into a bread tin (c. 35 cm long), well dusted with flour, cover and leave to rise for another 50 minutes. Place a bread-baking or pizza stone into the bottom of the oven, preheat the oven to 230°C (convection is best, or use 250°C top and bottom heat). Tip the bread on top of the stone, lightly brush the sides of the loaf with a water and sprinkle a good dash of water onto the base of the oven. Bake the bread for 15 minutes, then reduce the temperature to 190°C (210°C top and bottom heat) and bake for about 45 minutes until done. The bread is finished if you can hear a hollow sound when you tap on the bottom of the loaf. Take out of the oven and leave to cool completely.

ROOT VEGETABLE SOUP WITH CROÛTONS

Oh, what a wonderfully comforting hot soup, especially in autumn or winter. And the best thing about it is that you don't need a lot to fill you up. If you like, add a carrot; it will add a touch of sweetness.

COMFORTING AND WARMING

SERVES 4:

For the soup:

1 piece celeriac (c. 300 g)
150 g parsley roots
1 small white onion
2 tbsp butter
800 ml vegetable or chicken stock (ready-made or homemade, pp.32 or 59)
300 g cream
salt | freshly ground black pepper
cayenne pepper
freshly grated nutmeg

For the croûtons:

2 thick slices white spelt or wheat bread
2 tbsp butter

HOW LONG IT TAKES: c. 45 min
PER SERVING: c. 390 kcal | 5 g p | 33 g f | 16 g ch

1 To make the soup, peel and finely dice the celeriac, the parsley roots and the onion. Melt the butter in a large, wide saucepan. Add the onion and fry for about 3 minutes until translucent. Add the celeriac and the parsley root dice and fry for another 5 minutes. Pour in the vegetable or chicken stock, bring to the boil, then reduce the heat, cover and leave to simmer gently over low heat for 25 minutes.

2 Meanwhile, cut the bread into 1–1½ cm cubes. Melt the butter in a large frying pan. Add the bread cubes and fry over medium heat for about 3–4 minutes until golden and crisp. Take out of the pan and drain on kitchen paper.

3 Add the cream to the soup and simmer for another 5 minutes. Purée the soup with a handheld mixer until it is creamy and smooth. Bring to the boil again and season with salt, pepper, cayenne pepper and nutmeg. Divide the creamy root vegetable soup between warm deep plates, sprinkle with the croûtons and serve immediately.

USEFUL TIPS

For festive occasions, you can easily jazz up this soup and turn it into something a bit special. Cut 50 g of the fatty edge off a smoked goose or duck breast and cut into paper-thin, bite-sized slices. Arrange in the deep plates with the soup.

For an additional soup ingredient that's also a pretty decoration, using a potato peeler, peel 2 small parsley roots into thin strips or shave them into thin slices with a box grater. Heat 500–600 g deep-frying fat in a small, tall saucepan or deep-fryer. Add the parsley root strips or slices and deep-fry for 2–3 minutes until golden brown, then leave to drain briefly on kitchen paper. Lightly season with salt. Sprinkle the vegetable chips over the soup in the plates and serve immediately.

FRIED CARP IN BEER BATTER WITH SALAD

Carp is a favourite in Bavaria not only for Fridays, but also at Christmas or New Year's Eve. Whether fried as a whole fish, halved or served as a fillet, what's important for the best flavour is always the quality of the fish.

AUTHENTICALLY BAVARIAN

SERVES 4:

For the salad:

200 g floury potatoes | salt
100 g lamb's lettuce | 100 g curly endive lettuce
200 ml beef broth (p.52, or ready-made beef stock)
4 tbsp white vinegar
1 tsp sugar | a pinch of ground caraway seeds
freshly ground black pepper | 8 tbsp vegetable oil

For the fish:

8 fillets of carp (c. 90 g each, skinned, of a not-too-large carp)
2 eggs (medium) | salt
150 ml beer (e.g. lager) | 140 g flour
1 tbsp vegetable oil | 400 g clarified butter
freshly ground black pepper
freshly squeezed juice of ½ lemon

Plus: potato ricer

HOW LONG IT TAKES: c. 40 min

PER SERVING: c. 1540 kcal | 43 g p | 135 g f | 33 g ch

1 To make the salad, wash the potatoes and cook in salted water for 20–25 minutes until soft. Meanwhile, wash and spin-dry the lettuces. Remove the small roots from the lamb's lettuce, cut the curly endive into ½ cm strips. Using tweezers, remove any remaining bones from the carp fillets.

2 Drain the potatoes when done, pull off the skins and press the potatoes through a ricer. Heat the beef stock and stir with the vinegar into the potato purée. Season the potato dressing with salt, sugar, caraway seeds and pepper, then stir in the oil. Keep the dressing warm (e.g. in a water bath).

3 Separate the eggs. Beat the egg whites together with a pinch of salt until stiff. Lightly whisk the egg yolks with a dash of beer, then, a little at a time, stir in the flour, the remaining beer and finally the oil until you have a smooth batter. Fold in the beaten egg whites and lightly season the batter with salt.

4 Divide the clarified butter between two large frying pans and melt. Season the fish fillets with salt, pepper and lemon juice. Coat the fillets in the batter, one at a time, allow the surplus batter to drip off and then place the fish fillets into the hot fat. Fry for 2 minutes, turn carefully and fry for another 1 minute. Turn again and fry for another 1 minute until golden on both sides. Lift the fillets out of the pan and place on kitchen paper to drain.

5 Divide the lukewarm potato dressing between plates, arrange both types of salad on top. Add the carp fillets and serve.

USEFUL TIPS

Be careful when eating! Like a hake, the carp has hooked bones known as y-bones. They are very thin and are easily overlooked when removing the bones. Cooking time may vary depending on the thickness of the carp fillets: thicker pieces will take a little longer than thin ones. The fish is done when it still looks moist and glossy after frying.

TROUT FILLETS WITH CHARD

Bavaria has numerous lakes, ponds and streams which contain all sorts of creatures for a varied menu plan. Here we've fished out a trout. When it's well prepared it can easily hold its own against any saltwater fish.

CRISP AND JUICY

SERVES 4:

For the vegetables:

400 g red or white chard
1 small onion | 1½ tbsp cold butter
2 pinches of sugar | salt
300 ml vegetable stock | 100 g cream
freshly grated nutmeg
a dash of freshly squeezed lemon juice

For the fish:

8 trout fillets (c. 100 g each, with skin)
2 eggs (medium) | 3 tbsp flour
120 g almond flakes
freshly squeezed juice of ½ lemon
salt | freshly ground black pepper
6 tbsp clarified butter

HOW LONG IT TAKES: c. 1 hour
PER SERVING: c. 685 kcal | 46 g p | 50 g f | 10 g ch

1 To prepare the vegetables, wash and trim the chard. Cut the stems away from the leaves, halve thicker stems lengthways. Cut the stems into ½ cm pieces, roughly chop or tear the leaves. Peel and finely dice the onion.

2 In a saucepan, melt 1 tablespoon butter. Add the onion and fry for about 4 minutes until golden. Add the chard stems, season with sugar and salt and sauté for 5 minutes. Pour in 150 ml vegetable stock, cover and simmer over low heat for about 3 minutes. Stir in the chard leaves, pour in the remaining stock, cover and simmer for 10 minutes.

3 Meanwhile, prepare the fish. Using a tweezer, remove any remaining bones from the trout fillets. crack the eggs into a deep plate and whisk with a fork. Also put the flour and the almonds into separate deep plates.

4 Pour the cream onto the chard mixture and simmer for about 5 minutes until velvety. Just before serving, cut the remaining butter into small pats and stir them into the hot vegetables. Season with salt, pepper, nutmeg and lemon juice.

5 Meanwhile, season the trout fillets with lemon juice, salt and pepper, then turn them in the flour. Now pull only the fleshy sides through the egg and then press into the almonds. Heat the clarified butter in two large frying pans. Add the fillets, almond side down, and fry for about 3 minutes over medium heat until golden. Carefully turn the fillets and fry for about 1 minute on the skin side. Take the pans off the stove and leave the fillets to cook in the residual heat for about 3 minutes until the fat stops sizzling.

6 Arrange the chard mixture on warm plates with the crisply fried trout fillets and serve. Good with boiled potatoes.

USEFUL TIP

Leave the fillets of very freshly caught trout in the fridge for 1 day before frying, or they will curl up.

BAVARIANS AND THE CATHOLIC CHURCH

"OH HOLY TWINITY!"
(Karl Valentin)

A cunning, sometimes deeply black sense of humour and a penchant for all things odd, scurrilous and generally bizarre are typical Bavarian traits. How else can you explain how, in 1989, Bavaria's most famous, humorous carnival honours (named after the very popular comedian, the great late Karl Valentin) were conferred on none other than Cardinal Joseph Ratzinger who later became Pope Benedict XVI. He is a Bavarian himself, after all.

Karl Valentin, who coined his own German version of "Oh my dear God", is often said to have appreciated churches much more from the outside than ever from inside, if indeed at all (and Catholic ones even less so, having been raised a Protestant). Perhaps surprisingly, the comedian did, however, always keep two saints' pictures handy in his wallet: the Black Madonna of Altötting, and the image of a guardian angel guiding two children over a bridge.

And is it any wonder! After all, Bavaria is Catholic to the core: since the founding of the archdiocese of Freising in 739 – the bishopric's spiritual hub for some one thousand years – Catholicism has shaped everyday life to the same extent as politics and cuisine. The church is an integral part of every village. Statues of the Virgin Mary, Bavaria's patron saint, stand in every main market square – in Munich and in the other six bishoprics of Augsburg, Bamberg, Eichstätt, Passau, Regensburg and Würzburg. The state capital even borrowed its name from monks (which are known in German as "Mönche").

Christian holidays and rituals serve as the cornerstones of the calendar year. On Mariä Lichtmess, or Candlemas (2 February), for example, many churches consecrate candles for the year ahead. In the alpine uplands, many families today still gather to pray the Rosary, lighting a candle for each family member, the flames representing their futures. After the wild carnival celebrations, Ash Wednesday marks the start of Lent. To this day, priests use ash to draw the sign of the cross on the foreheads of the faithful as a symbol of penance and cleansing. People fast in accordance with the rules of Christianity until Easter Saturday, usually eating only bread, water and fish – the latter a symbol of the Early Church. A number of Catholic households incidentally also replace meat with fish on Fridays as a means of reflecting on Jesus' crucifixion every week, rather than just on Good Friday. And so the year continues with numerous festivities reflecting rural customs and a deep-rooted faith – from Ascension Day through Erntedank (German harvest thanksgiving) to Advent. Karl Valentin was acutely aware that, generally, the Bavarians had things a lot better than even many heavenly angels. As he summed it up, "Simply flying around in the afterlife for eternity doing nothing more than sing Hosanna (as we know from the Bible) may be well and good for the first eight days, but the thought of doing it forever – that's got to be boring."

MUSHROOM AND PARSLEY RAGOUT

You can smell a mushroom, say the Bavarians! And in the autumn, when the weather is right, they are packed by a fever: off they go to the woods mushroom-hunting! Usually you'd be on your own, or out with a friend, for the spots where mushrooms have found an ideal forest floor are well-treasured secrets. Everyone else just follows their nose.

UNBEATABLY DELICIOUS

SERVES 4:

1 large onion | 1 garlic clove
1 bay leaf | 2 cloves
90 g clarified butter | 50 g flour
800 ml milk | 300 g cream
850 g mixed mushrooms (e.g. chanterelles, boletes, ceps, button mushrooms or common field mushrooms)
salt | ¼ l vegetable stock
freshly ground black pepper
freshly grated nutmeg
a pinch of finely grated organic lemon zest
2–3 sprigs flat-leaved parsley

HOW LONG IT TAKES: c. 1 hour 10 min
PER SERVING: c. 650 kcal | 16 g p | 54 g f | 23 g ch

1 Peel the onion and the garlic. Halve the onion and attach the bay leaf to one onion half by sticking it into place with the cloves. Finely dice the other onion half and the garlic.

2 In a small saucepan, melt 50 g clarified butter, add the flour and stir until smooth. Add the milk, a little at a time, stirring all the time – best done using a whisk – until smooth. Bring the béchamel sauce to the boil, then simmer for 5–6 minutes over low heat. Add the studded onion half and simmer the sauce for another 12 minutes, stirring frequently so it doesn't burn or stick to the saucepan. Stir in 200 g cream and simmer for another 8 minutes.

3 Meanwhile, trim the mushrooms and rub them with a moistened kitchen towel to clean, then halve larger mushrooms or cut them into ½ cm slices. In a large frying pan, melt a little clarified butter, then add and fry the mushrooms – sorted by type – over high heat for 3 minutes, season lightly with salt, then take out of the pan. Don't fry too many mushrooms at a time, they will lose too much water.

4 Melt the remaining butter in the pan, add the onion and garlic dice and fry for 3 minutes. Pour in the vegetable stock and bring to the boil. Add the mushrooms and the béchamel sauce to the onion stock and bring everything to the boil again. Season with salt, pepper, nutmeg and lemon zest.

5 Whisk the remaining cream with a handheld mixer until smooth, then stir it into the mushroom ragout. Rinse and shake dry the parsley, pull off and roughly chop the leaves. Stir the parsley into the ragout. Divide the mushroom ragout between warm deep plates and serve with bread dumplings (p.89).

USEFUL TIP

The mushrooms in the shops vary according to the season. It starts with chanterelles in June, followed from mid-June to October by ceps. Boletes are available from July/August. Cultivated mushrooms like button mushrooms are sold all year round.

SPINACH WITH EGG AND CHANTERELLES

Spinach and egg are a classic Friday dish. Cook-of-the-century Eckart Witzigmann elevated this dish into the gourmet heaven, refining it even more with fresh white truffles. In this version, we serve the aromatic spinach with fried chanterelle mushrooms.

CLASSIC AND GOOD

SERVES 4:
1 kg young leaf spinach
salt | 1 onion
1 large garlic clove
400 g chanterelles
5 tbsp butter | 200 g cream
freshly ground black pepper
freshly grated nutmeg
a pinch of sugar
1 tsp clarified butter
2 pinches of ground caraway seeds
8 eggs (medium)

HOW LONG IT TAKES: c. 1 hour
PER SERVING: c. 470 kcal | 22 g p | 40 g f | 5 g ch

1 Thoroughly wash and trim the leaf spinach. Put the spinach into boiling salted water and cook for 3 minutes. Drain the spinach in a sieve and rinse under cold water to stop it cooking. Squeeze the spinach with your hands until no more liquid escapes. Now, in small portions, put the spinach into a narrow, tall container. Finely purée with a hand blender – this allows the spinach to stay a bright and luminous green colour (puréeing larger quantities would also take too long).

2 Peel the onion and the garlic. Finely dice the onion. Cut 2 thin slices off the garlic and finely dice the rest. Carefully trim the mushrooms and rub with a moistened kitchen paper towel to clean. Cut larger mushrooms in half.

3 In a large, wide saucepan, melt 2 tablespoons of butter. Add the onion and garlic cubes and fry over medium heat for about 2 minutes. Pour in the cream and bring to the boil. Season with salt, pepper and nutmeg and simmer for another 2 minutes until creamy. Stir in the spinach and cook for 2 minutes. Add 1 tablespoon of butter in small pats, as well as the sugar, and simmer everything for 5–6 minutes over low heat, stirring from time to time. Set the spinach aside and keep warm.

4 Meanwhile, melt the clarified butter in a large frying pan. Add the chanterelles and cook over high heat for 6–7 minutes, allowing any escaping liquid to completely boil away. Add the garlic slices and cook the mushrooms for another 3 minutes. Season with salt, pepper and caraway seeds.

5 Melt the remaining butter in two large frying pans, add a little salt. Crack the eggs into a cup, then slide them carefully into the pans, one at a time, and fry for about 4 minutes over low to medium heat. The eggs are perfect when the egg whites have set without a brown edge and the egg yolks are soft and run when pricked with a fork.

6 If preferred, purée the spinach again with the hand blender, check the seasoning. Arrange the creamy spinach with the fried eggs and the mushrooms on warm plates and serve. Boiled potatoes are particularly delicious with this dish.

CHEESE SPAETZLE AND ONION BAKE

Juicy, aromatic and baked to a golden brown – that's a proper cheese spaetzle dish. Depending on your region, the spaetzle are finished with a delicious cheese sauce in the oven or in the frying pan.

FOR BAVARIAN GIRLS AND BOYS

SERVES 4:

For the spaetzle:

300 g spaetzle flour or plain white flour
5 eggs (medium) | 4 egg yolks (medium)
salt | freshly grated nutmeg
50 g Weißlacker (a pungent cheese from the Allgäu, known as beer cheese, optional)
200 g mildly aromatic alpine cheese
350 g onions | 4 tbsp butter
freshly ground black pepper
200 g cream | 100 ml vegetable stock
1 bunch chives

For the roast onions:

1 kg deep-frying fat
1½ large onions
1½ tbsp flour
1 level tsp sweet paprika

Plus: spaetzle maker or ricer
aluminium foil

HOW LONG IT TAKES: c. 1 hour 30 min
PER SERVING: c. 950 kcal | 38 g p | 60 g f | 65 g ch

1 To make the spaetzle, put the flour, eggs, egg yolks, 2 tablespoons of cold water, salt and nutmeg into the bowl of a food processor and process for about 10 minutes until you have a smooth, thick dough. Grate or press the dough, a little at a time, into plenty of boiling salted water, bring to the boil and simmer briefly. Lift the spaetzle out of the water using a slotted spoon, put them into a sieve, rinse under cold water and leave to drain. (You can find more details for the preparation on p.93.)

2 Crumble the Weißlacker, finely grate the alpine cheese. Peel the onions and cut into ½ cm cubes. In a large frying pan, melt 2 tablespoons of butter. Add the onion cubes and fry over medium heat for 12–13 minutes until golden. Now add the remaining butter and the spaetzle, warm through for 3 minutes. Season with salt, pepper and nutmeg. Combine the cream and vegetable stock, bring to the boil.

3 Preheat the oven to 150°C (best convection, otherwise 170°C top and bottom heat). Layer the spaetzle and onion mixture alternately with the cheese into a gratin dish or a roaster (c. 18 x 30 cm), finishing with cheese. Pour the creamy stock over the spaetzle, cover with aluminium foil and bake in the oven (centre) for about 20 minutes. Take off the foil, raise the oven temperature to 200°C (convection, 220°C top and bottom heat) and bake the spaetzle for 12–14 minutes until golden brown.

4 Meanwhile, in a tall saucepan, heat the deep-frying fat for the fried onions (160–170°C). Peel the onions, then cut them into thin rings and combine with the flour and the paprika. Put the onion rings in several batches into the hot fat and deep-fry for about 2 minutes until golden and leave to drain on kitchen paper. (You can find more details for the preparation on p.77.)

5 Rinse and shake dry the chives, then snip them into fine rings. Remove the cheese spaetzle from the oven, garnish with the roasted onions and chives and serve. This dish is particularly delicious with a mixed leaf salad.

POTATO CRUMBLE WITH SOURED MILK

In times gone by, mothers and housewives excelled at making something really delicious from a few ingredients. This crumble made from cooked potatoes is definitely one of those miracle dishes and is sure to excite your tastebuds too.

NOW FOR SOMETHING REALLY EASY

SERVES 4:

1 kg floury potatoes
salt
150 g flour
80 g clarified butter
800 g buttermilk

HOW LONG IT TAKES: c. 35 min
IN THE OVEN: c. 50 min
PER SERVING: c. 565 kcal | 15 g p | 27 g f | 64 g ch

1 Wash the potatoes, then boil them in salted water for 20–25 minutes until soft. Drain, leave them to steam for a little, slip off the skins and leave to cool completely. Mash the potatoes with your fingers and spread evenly onto the work surface, then sift over the flour. Work both together with your hands until you have large crumbs.

2 Preheat the oven to 180°C (convection is best, or 200°C top and bottom heat). Melt the clarified butter in a roasting pan. Evenly spread the potato crumbs in the dish. Bake in the oven (centre) for 35 minutes, then turn them using a spatula and cook for another 15 minutes until golden brown and crisp.

3 Take the pan out of the oven and put it straight onto the table. Serve with the soured milk. Instead of soured milk, you could also use sauerkraut (p.202) as an accompaniment for the crumble. For a sweet-toothed variation, you could also serve it with apple compote (see right).

USEFUL TIPS

Make sure the potatoes have cooled completely before continuing to work with them. If the potatoes are still hot, they will not produce delicate crumbs but a tough and gooey mixture.
Instead of buttermilk, you can use soured milk. To make soured milk, combine 750 g milk with 45 g lemon juice or vinegar and leave to stand for 5 minutes before use.
To serve 2, the crumble can also be made in the frying pan. Simply cook 500 g potatoes, mash them and work them into crumbs with 75 g flour. Melt 60 g clarified butter in a large frying pan, add the crumbs and fry for about 10 minutes over medium heat until golden brown, stirring occasionally.

GOOD WITH: APPLE COMPOTE

Quarter and peel 500 g tart apples (e.g. Pink Lady or Cox), remove the cores and cut into about ½ cm wedges. In a saucepan, caramelize 1 tablespoon of brown sugar over medium heat until light in colour, pour in 100 ml water and bring to the boil. Add the apples to the saucepan. Slit open ¼ vanilla pod lengthways and scrape out the seeds. Add both pod and seeds with 2 small pieces of cinnamon stick to the apples. Cover and cook for 5–6 minutes until soft. Leave the apple compote to cool a little, then serve with the potato crumble.

YEAST DUMPLINGS WITH A CRUST

You'll need to use your instincts to get the dough, temperature and cooking time just right to make perfect yeast dumplings. Cooking without instinct just doesn't work!

FLUFFY ON TOP, CRISPY BELOW

SERVES 4:

For the yeast dumplings:
500 g flour | 80 g sugar
200 ml milk | 1 cube yeast (42 g)
100 g butter | 2 eggs (medium)
salt | 80 g clarified butter
flour for working

For the sauce:
1 vanilla pod | 600 ml milk
6 egg yolks (medium) | 80 g sugar
a pinch of ground cinnamon

HOW LONG IT TAKES: c. 1 hour
RESTING: c. 1 hour 15 min
PER SERVING: c. 1230 kcal | 30 g p | 61 g f | 141 g ch

1 Put the flour into the bowl of a food processor (or work with a mixing bowl and a handheld mixer) and make a well in the centre. Sprinkle the sugar around the edge. Heat the milk to lukewarm. Spoon 5 tablespoons of milk into a cup, crumble in the yeast, add 1 tablespoon of flour (from the bowl) and stir well to combine. Pour the mixture into the well in the bowl. Cover and leave in a warm place for 20 minutes.

2 Roughly dice the butter and add to the remaining milk with the eggs (without stirring!). Add the eggs, milk and a pinch of salt to the mixture. Work everything with the kneading hooks until you have a smooth, bubbling dough. Dust your hands and the work surface with flour, lift the dough out of the bowl and shape it into a ball. Dust the inside of the bowl with flour, place the yeast dough in the bowl, cover and leave to rise for a further 20 minutes. Knead the dough again on the floured work surface, cover and leave to rise for another 20 minutes.

3 Knead the yeast dough again on the work surface, divide it into 8 even-sized pieces and shape these into balls. Place the dough balls on a floured wooden board, cover and leave to rise for another 15 minutes.

4 Brush a large saucepan (28 cm diameter) with clarified butter, then pour in 400 ml lukewarm water and add a pinch of salt. Place the dough balls side by side in the saucepan. Cover the saucepan first with a kitchen towel (to absorb the water that will condense), then with a lid. Cook the yeast dumplings for 35–40 minutes on the stove over medium heat until they have risen and have a nice, golden brown crust at the bottom. Under no circumstance remove the lid or else the dumplings will collapse! Leave to stand briefly, then remove the lid and the towel.

5 Meanwhile, to make the sauce, slit the vanilla pod lengthways and scrape out the seeds. Put both the pod and the seeds into the milk and bring to the boil. Take the milk off the stove. In a metal bowl (if possible, use one with a rounded base), beat the egg yolks and the sugar with a whisk until smooth. Gradually add and stir in the hot milk. Stir the vanilla and egg milk over a waterbath until you have a thickish custard sauce (takes about 10–15 minutes). Remove the vanilla pod and discard. Flavour the sauce with cinnamon, leave to cool a little and serve with the yeast dumplings.

SEMOLINA BAKE WITH CHERRIES

Bavarians have a sweet tooth and they quite enjoy eating their sweet dishes as a main course.

LIGHT AND FRUITY

SERVES 4:

300 g sour cherries (Morello)
1 vanilla pod
80 g butter
400 ml milk
100 g cream
a pinch of finely grated zest of an organic orange
a pinch of finely grated zest of an organic lemon
125 g semolina
4 eggs (medium)
a pinch of salt
50 g sugar
2 heaped tbsp icing sugar
1 tsp butter and 1 tbsp sugar for
the dish or roasting pan

HOW LONG IT TAKES: c. 30 min
IN THE OVEN: c. 40 min
PER SERVING: c. 610 kcal | 15 g p | 37 g f | 54 g ch

1 Wash and pick over the cherries. Remove the stalks and the stones. Slit the vanilla pod lengthways and scrape out the seeds.

2 Put the butter into a saucepan together with the milk, cream, vanilla seeds and vanilla pod, as well as the orange and lemon zest. Bring everything to the boil, then gradually drizzle in the semolina and cook, stirring constantly, over medium heat for 3–4 minutes. Remove the vanilla pod and discard, transfer the semolina mixture to a bowl and leave to cool for about 10 minutes until lukewarm, stirring from time to time.

3 Separate the eggs. Using the whisks of a handheld mixer, beat the egg whites with the salt and sugar until stiff. Beat the egg yolks with 1 heaped tablespoon of icing sugar for about 3 minutes until light and frothy. Stir the egg yolk mixture into the semolina mixture until smooth, then carefully fold in the egg white mixture using a dough scraper.

4 Preheat the oven to 200°C. Brush an ovenproof dish or a roasting pan (c. 18 x 28 cm) with butter and sprinkle with sugar – make sure the edges are also well covered with the butter and the sugar. Pour one third of the semolina mixture into the dish or pan, then place one third of the cherries on top. Add another third of semolina and of cherries. Finally add the remaining semolina, finishing with the cherries.

5 Put the semolina bake into the oven (centre, convection 180°C) and bake for about 40 minutes until golden brown. Take the finished bake out of the oven, while still hot dust with the remaining icing sugar and serve immediately or leave to cool to lukewarm before serving.

USEFUL TIP

When cherries are not in season you can also use frozen cherries, or even cherries preserved in a jar. Simply layer the frozen cherries without defrosting, or the well-drained preserved cherries in the dish with the semolina mixture and then bake the dish as described above.

PANCAKES WITH HOMEMADE JAM

Savoury or sweet – everyone loves pancakes!

A FAVOURITE WITH YOUNG AND OLD

MAKES ABOUT 8 LARGE PANCAKES AND 6 JARS OF JAM:

For the jam:
500 g rhubarb
500 g strawberries
½ vanilla pod
½ organic lemon
500 g jam sugar (2:1)

For the pancakes:
240 g flour
400 ml milk
8 eggs (medium)
a pinch of salt
1 tbsp sugar
8 tbsp vegetable oil
icing sugar for dusting (if liked)

Plus:
6 screw-top jars (200 ml contents each)

HOW LONG IT TAKES: c. 20 min (jam) and c. 30 min (pancakes)

PER PORTION (PANCAKE):
c. 320 kcal | 12 g p | 18 g f | 28 g ch

PER JAR (JAM):
c. 365 kcal | 1 g p | 0 g f | 87 g ch

1 To make the jam, wash the rhubarb and cut off the woody stem ends and the green leaves. Pull off any strings that show. Halve thick stems lengthways, then cut the rhubarb into 1½–2 cm pieces. Wash and trim the strawberries, then halve or quarter them depending on their size. Slit the vanilla pod lengthways, scrape out the seeds. Wash the lemon under hot water and pat dry, then finely grate off the zest and squeeze out 2 tablespoons of juice. Put everything into a saucepan with the sugar and stir well to combine.

2 Gradually bring the fruit mixture to the boil, stirring constantly, then cook for 3 minutes over medium heat. Using a handheld mixer, purée lightly and cook for another 1 minute. Pour the boiling hot jam into thoroughly cleaned jars. Close with the lids, turn upside down and leave to rest for 3–4 minutes. Turn the jars the right way up and leave the jam to cool. Store in the fridge or a cool place.

3 Preheat the oven to 100°C (use top and bottom heat, convection is not recommended). To make the pancakes, put the flour into a bowl. Gradually add the milk, stirring with a whisk. Whisk in the eggs until you have a smooth, runny batter. Season with salt and sugar and leave to rise for 10 minutes.

4 Heat a little oil in a large frying pan (28 cm diameter, nonstick is best). Pour in 1 ladleful of batter, spreading the batter evenly by shaking the pan. Bake the pancake batter over medium heat for about 1 minute until golden brown, then turn it using a spatula and bake the second side for about 1 minute until also golden brown. Lift the pancake out of the pan and place it on a heatproof platter and keep warm in the oven. Make more pancakes with the remaining batter as described and keep them warm in the oven until serving.

5 Thinly spread the pancakes with the rhubarb and strawberry jam, then roll up or fold over. If liked, dust with a little icing sugar and serve.

LOVELY LEFTOVERS

Bavarians don't like letting things go to waste! And so, rather than into the bin, any leftovers go into the next dish, beautifully pepped up and complemented by other ingredients – cheap and cheerful.

FARMHOUSE FRY-UP

This hearty pan-fry of beans, crisply fried potatoes and yesterday's leftover roast pork is as delicious in summer as it is in winter. And it doesn't even look like leftovers!

HEARTY AND SUBSTANTIAL

SERVES 2:
100 g runner beans
salt
60 g smoked pork belly
½ onion
½ garlic clove
250 g cold cooked pork roast (p.71)
300 g cold potatoes, boiled in their skins
1 tbsp clarified butter
freshly ground black pepper
a pinch of caraway seeds
2 sprigs flat-leaved parsley
1 sprig marjoram

HOW LONG IT TAKES: c. 35 min
PER SERVING: c. 400 kcal | 37 g p | 17 g f | 25 g ch

1 Wash and trim the runner beans, then cut off the stem ends. Pull any strings that can be seen. Cut the beans into 2 cm lengths. Bring plenty of salted water to the boil, add the beans and cook for about 7 minutes until al dente. Drain in a sieve and rinse in ice-cold water to stop cooking, then leave to drain well (see tips).

2 Meanwhile, cut the pork belly into not-too-small cubes. Peel the onion and cut it into 1 cm cubes, peel and finely chop the garlic. Cut the roast pork into 2 cm cubes. Peel the potatoes and cut them into about 1 cm slices.

3 In a large frying pan, melt the clarified butter. Spread the potato slices side by side in the pan and fry over medium heat for 1 minute. Add the pork belly and continue frying for another 2 minutes, until the potatoes are golden. Turn the potato slices, add the onion and fry for another 3 minutes. Add the roast pork and the garlic and fry everything for another 2 minutes, stirring occassionally. Finally stir in the beans and heat through for about ½ minute. Season with salt, pepper and caraway seeds.

4 Rinse and shake dry the parsley and the marjoram, pull off and roughly chop the leaves. Sprinkle the herbs into the pan, shake to combine and serve. If you have a few spoonfuls of leftover roast pork meat stock (p.71) or rich meat stock (p.76) – that would make this country fry-up just perfect.

USEFUL TIPS

The cooking time may vary slightly depending on the type of beans you are using. It's better therefore to check the beans for doneness from time to time. The beans should under no circumstance "squeak" when you bite into them.

After cooking, make sure you immediately rinse or immerse the beans in ice-cold water; this will stop the cooking process and preserve the lovely green colour of the beans.

If you happen to have some fresh savory at home, put 1 sprig into the water when cooking the beans. This highly aromatic herb beautifully underlines the flavour of the beans.

ROAST GOOSE FRY-UP WITH APPLE

QUICK AND TASTY

SERVES 2:

250 g cold roast goose
(leg or breast, p.180)
2 cold cooked potato dumplings
(c. 350 g, p.88)
1 onion
½ apple (e.g. Cox's Orange Pippin)
1½ tbsp goose fat
a pinch of dried mugwort (if liked)
salt | freshly ground black pepper

HOW LONG IT TAKES: c. 20 min
PER SERVING: c. 475 kcal | 31 g p | 23 g f | 34 g ch

1 Cut the goose into about 2 cm pieces. Halve the dumplings, then cut into about 1 cm thick slices. Peel and finely dice the onion. Wash the apple (peel it if you prefer), then halve and remove the core. Also cut the apple into small cubes.

2 In a large frying pan, heat 1 tablespoon of goose fat. Add the dumplings and fry for 2 minutes over high heat. Turn over, add the onion and fry for another 2 minutes. Stir in the remaining fat and the meat and fry for 1 minute. Add the apple cubes and the mugwort, if using, and fry for another 5 minutes. Season with salt and pepper, arrange on plates. If you have some goose stock left over (p.180), bring to the boil and drizzle over the goose. Serve.

GOOD WITH: RED CABBAGE SALAD

In a saucepan, caramelize 1 tablespoon of sugar to light brown. Add 150 g slices quince, pour in 100 ml apple juice, cover and simmer for 5 minutes over low heat, leave to cool. Combine 350 g finely slices red cabbage with 3 tablespoons of cider vinegar, season with salt and pepper, combine well and leave to marinate for 15 minutes. Drain the quince and stir into the cabbage together with 3 tablespoons of grape seed oil. Season the salad with a pinch each of ground cinnamon and allspice.

CRISPY DUMPLING WITH EGG

Bavaria without dumplings is like a winter without snow. And to make sure this does not occur people come up with all sorts of ideas. Thus, for example, leftover dumplings are fried up – often with yesterday's meat and onions – making for a hearty main course.

QUICK AND INEXPENSIVE

SERVES 2:

400 g cold cooked bread dumplings, serviette dumplings or pretzel dumplings (pp.89–91)
½ onion
1 spring onion
1 large sprig flat-leaved parsley
2 eggs (medium)
2 tbsp butter
salt | freshly ground black pepper
freshly grated nutmeg
a pinch of ground caraway seeds
100 ml beef stock (p.52, or ready-made beef stock)
1 tbsp medium-hot mustard
1 tsp sweet Bavarian mustard
50 g cream

HOW LONG IT TAKES: c. 20 min
PER SERVING: c. 865 kcal | 16 g p | 29 g f | 21 g ch

1 Halve the dumplings and cut into ½ cm slices. Peel and finely dice the onion. Wash and trim the spring onion, then cut it diagonally into thin rings. Rinse and shake dry the parsley, pull off the leaves, reserving a few, roughly chop the rest. In a bowl, stir the eggs to combine well.

2 Melt the butter in a large frying pan. Add the dumplings and fry over medium heat for 1 minute. Add the onion and the white parts of the spring onion and fry for 4 minutes. Sprinkle in the green parts of the spring onion, fry for 2 minutes. Season with salt, pepper, nutmeg and caraway seeds. Pour in the egg and sprinkle the chopped parsley over the dumplings and leave to set for 30 seconds, stirring frequently. Keep warm.

3 Meanwhile, in a small saucepan, bring the beef stock to the boil with the two types of mustard, stirring constantly. Stir in the cream, bring back to the boil, simmer for about 2 minutes over medium heat until velvety. Season with salt and pepper. Arrange the dumplings on plates with the sauce, sprinkle over the remaining parsley and serve.

USEFUL TIP

To make a more substantial version, cut 50 g smoked pork belly into small cubes, then add them to the dumplings with the onion.

GOOD WITH: LAMB'S LETTUCE WITH BEETROOT DRESSING

Peel and finely dice ½ small onion and fry in 1 tablespoon vegetable oil for 2 minutes until translucent. Pour in 2 tablespoons of cider vinegar and 50 ml vegetable stock. Season with ½ teaspoon sugar, salt and pepper, bring to the boil and take off the stove. Peel and finely dice 50 g cooked beetroot, put into a small bowl. Pour over the hot dressing, add a pinch of ground caraway seeds, stir in 3 tablespoons of vegetable oil and leave the dressing for 30 minutes for the flavours to develop. Wash and trim 100 g lamb's lettuce, combine with the dressing.

You can find finger gnocchi at Christmas markets and medieval fairs.
Giant frying pans give off the delicious smell of this popular southern German speciality,
which is served not only as a side dish but also on its own, savoury or sweet.

FINGER GNOCCHI WITH SAUERKRAUT

HEARTY AND INEXPENSIVE

SERVES 2:

80 g smoked pork belly
1–2 tsp clarified butter
250 g cooked finger gnocchi (p.93)
400 g cooked sauerkraut (p.202)
2 tbsp cream
salt | freshly ground black pepper
1–2 pinches of ground caraway seeds

HOW LONG IT TAKES: c. 15 min
PER SERVING: c. 280 kcal | 13 g p | 18 g f | 13 g ch

1 Cut the pork belly into strips about 4 cm long and ½ cm wide. Put the belly strips with the clarified butter into a large cold frying pan, set on top of the stove and warm through gradually over low heat, cooking the pork belly for 4–5 minutes.

2 Add the finger gnocchi to the pan and fry for 2 minutes. Stir in the sauerkraut and warm through for about 3 minutes. Add the cream, season with salt, pepper and caraway seeds. Serve the finger gnocchi and sauerkraut straight from the pan.

USEFUL TIP

By putting the pork in a cold frying pan and only then turning on the heat, it will be fried slowly and stay crisp without drying out. This also works for bacon. Depending on how fatty the bacon is you will need 1–2 tablespoons clarified butter or vegetable oil.

OR TRY THIS:

Instead of using homemade sauerkraut in this recipe you can also use a ready-made 3-minute tinned sauerkraut and ready-made Italian gnocchi from the chiller cabinet.

FINGER GNOCCHI WITH VANILLA BUTTER

SWEET AND SWIFT

SERVES 2:

2 tbsp butter
2 tsp ground poppy seeds
200 g cooked finger gnocchi (p.93)
2 tsp vanilla sugar (see tip)

HOW LONG IT TAKES: c. 5 min
PER SERVING: c. 170 kcal | 3 g p | 11 g f | 14 g ch

1 In a large frying pan, melt the butter until frothy. Stir in the poppy seeds and leave to cook briefly. Add the finger gnocchi and fry for about 1 minute over medium heat. Sprinkle over the vanilla sugar and fry for another 1 minute. This colours the butter and gives it a slightly nutty flavour.

2 Serve the hot gnocchi with the poppy seed butter on plates or straight from the pan.

USEFUL TIP

A vanilla pod still has plenty of aroma even after the seeds have been scraped out. Therefore, don't throw it away but use it instead to make your own vanilla sugar. Simply stick the vanilla pod into a screw-top jar, cover it with sugar, close the jar and leave to stand for a few days. This allows the sugar to absorb the flavour of the vanilla pod. In order to further intensify the vanilla aroma, you can repeatedly add new vanilla pods to the sugar. Homemade vanilla sugar is a great product and guaranteed to be better than the shop-bought variety. In a pretty jar, it would even make a nice culinary present.

BREAD-WRAPPED MEAT LOAF

You may think you don't need a recipe to fry up some Bavarian meat loaf. But how about slices of loaf-shaped sausage cleverly stuffed and then wrapped in crunchy bread?

CLEVER YET DOWN TO EARTH

SERVES 4:

4 slices Bavarian loaf sausage or Bologna sausage (c. 170 g each and 2 cm thick)
8 tsp Bavarian sweet mustard
8 large, paperthin slices of farmhouse bread (c. 20 g each)
4 tbsp soft butter
2 sprigs flat-leaved parsley
a few chive stems
4 eggs (medium)
salt | freshly ground black pepper

HOW LONG IT TAKES: c. 20 min
PER SERVING:
c. 730 kcal | 39 g p | 56 g f | 19 g ch

1 Halve the meat loaf slices crossways, place them onto the work surface and cut a pocket into each half. Spread the insides of the pockets with 1 teaspoon of mustard each and lightly press the cut sides together. Spread each of the bread slices with 1 teaspoon of butter, place the meat loaf on top and wrap in the bread, pressing the bread onto the filling. Rinse and shake dry the herbs, pull off and finely chop the parsley leaves and snip the chives into thin rings.

2 Preheat the oven to 120°C (use top and bottom heat, convection is not recommended). Melt the remaining butter in two large frying pans. Add the bread parcels and fry over medium heat for about 2 minutes, then turn and fry for another 3 minutes. Frequently turn the parcels while cooking until they are crisp all over. Transfer the parcels to a baking tray and keep them warm in the oven (centre).

3 Crack the eggs into a cup, then let them slide, one at a time, into the two frying pans. Sprinkle with the parsley, then season to taste with salt and pepper. Cook for about 2–3 minutes to allow the eggs to set. Place the meat loaf parcels onto warm plates and put an egg on each plate. Sprinkle with the snipped chives and serve immediately.

HAM-AND-QUAIL'S EGG TOASTIES

The gentrified version of simple home cooking, this noble finger food is a real eye-catcher.

SOMETHING SPECIAL

SERVES 4:

120 g ham (thin slices)
12 slices rye bread from a small tin loaf
some salad leaves for the garnish
(e.g. lamb's lettuce or curly endive)
2 tbsp butter
salt
12 quail's eggs
freshly ground black pepper

Plus:

metal rings or biscuit cutters
(c. 5 cm diameter)

HOW LONG IT TAKES: c. 15 min

PER SERVING:

c. 250 kcal | 14 g p | 9 g f | 26 g ch

1 Cut the ham to fit the size of the bread slices, cover and chill until use. Rinse and pat dry the salad leaves, tear larger leaves into smaller pieces, set aside.

2 Gradually melt a little butter in a large frying pan. Add the bread slices and fry over medium heat for 1 minute each, then turn and fry for another 1 minute. Take out of the pan and drain on kitchen paper.

3 Lightly season the butter in the pan with salt. With a knife, carefully cut open the quail's eggs, one at a time, into a cup. Place the ring cutter into the pan and slide an egg it into the ring cutter in the frying pan, cook to set and remove the cutter. Repeat for all the eggs, cooking each egg for about 2 minutes.

4 Arrange the bread slices on small plates, cover with lettuce leaves and ham slices and place a quail's egg on each one. Grind over some black pepper and serve.

USEFUL TIP

If you cannot find a small tin loaf, simply use a larger loaf and cut the slices to suit.

BEEF SALAD WITH CAULIFLOWER

A fantastic summer dish, combining the best ingredients of a homemade broth!

SOPHISTICATED AND ELEGANT

SERVES 2:

1 egg (medium)
100 g cauliflower florets
salt
300 g cold cooked beef (e.g. boiled fillet, brisket or flat ribs)
100 g each cooked carrots and cooked celeriac (from cooking the boiled fillet or from making a broth)
½ bunch chives
100 ml beef broth (e.g. of boiled fillet, ready-made beef stock or beef broth, p.52)
2 tbsp white wine vinegar
2 tbsp cider vinegar
a pinch of sugar
freshly ground black pepper
2 tbsp grape seed oil (or sunflower oil)
2 tsp horseradish (from the jar)

HOW LONG IT TAKES: c. 30 min
PER SERVING: c. 460 kcal | 44 g p | 26 g f | 8 g ch

1 Put the egg into boiling water and cook for about 10 minutes until hard-boiled. Drain and rinse the egg under cold water, shell it and cut it into small cubes. Put the cauliflower florets into a saucepan with plenty of boiling salted water and cook for about 5–6 minutes until tender. Drain the cauliflower in a sieve and also rinse under ice-cold water.

2 Meanwhile, using a sharp knife, slice the cooked beef as thinly as possible. Dice the cooked carrots and the celeriac. Rinse and shake dry the chives and snip them into thin rings.

3 Heat the beef broth to lukewarm, add the carrot and celeriac dice and warm through. Stir the white wine vinegar, cider vinegar, sugar, salt and pepper into the broth, adding the oil right at the end. Combine the cauliflower florets and the egg cubes with the dressing.

4 Place the meat slices on plates and cover with the vegetable dressing. Sprinkle with the chives and grind over some pepper. Add 1 teaspoon of horseradish to each plate, then serve the beef salad. Good with country bread.

A GOOD BASE: BOILED BEEF

In a large saucepan, bring about 3 litres water to the boil. Lightly season 750 g topside beef (sinews and fatty parts removed) with salt, put into a frying pan with 2 tablespoons vegetable oil, fry for 3 minutes all over, then transfer to the boiling water. Also add 3 soup bones and 1 marrowbone. Bring everything to the boil, lifting off the scum from time to time, then simmer the meat over low heat for 1 hour. Peel and halve 2 carrots, 1 piece celeriac (c. 300 g) and 1 onion. Trim and wash 1 leek (c. 80 g), rinse 6–8 sprigs parsley. Add the vegetables and the parsley to the saucepan together with 1 lightly crushed garlic clove, 1 teaspoon each of black peppercorns, juniper berries and allspice berries as well as 2 bay leaves. Cook everything for another 2 hours–2 hours 30 minutes until tender. Lift the meat and the vegetables out of the broth, strain the broth through a sieve. Prepare, for example, as beef salad (above) or enjoy with fresh horseradish or swedes (p.82). The boiled beef broth can also be cooled and frozen in portions for later use.

PRETZEL SALAD WITH RADISH AND CHEESE

It's well known that Bavarians and Italians are soul mates. Both have a high regard for amazing concoctions made from the simplest of ingredients. This Bavarian version of the Italian panzanella bread salad is one such marvel.

EASY AND INEXPENSIVE

SERVES 4:

3 young red long radishes
1 small cucumber
2 sticks celery
180 g mild alpine cheese (without rind)
4 stale large pretzel breadsticks (1–2 days old)
60 g butter
150 ml vegetable stock
4 tbsp white wine vinegar
4 tbsp cider vinegar
2 tsp sugar
salt | freshly ground black pepper
5 tbsp grape seed oil (or sunflower oil)
½ bunch chives

HOW LONG IT TAKES: c. 30 min
PER SERVING: c. 560 kcal | 18 g p | 40 g f | 31 g ch

1 Thoroughly scrub the radishes under running water using a vegetable brush, halve them lengthways and then shave or cut them crossways into 3 mm slices. Wash the cucumber and peel it so that green strips of peel remain. Quarter the cucumber lengthways, cut out the seeds, halve the cucumber pieces again lengthways, then cut them diagonally into 1½ cm chunks. Wash and trim the celery, halve lengthways, then cut them diagonally into ½ cm chunks. Finely dice the cheese.

2 Halve the breadsticks lengthways, then cut them into 1½-cm wide pieces. Melt the butter in a large frying pan. Add the pretzel pieces and fry over medium heat for 4–5 minutes until golden all over. Take out of the pan and drain on kitchen paper.

3 Heat the vegetable stock to lukewarm, stir in the white wine vinegar, cider vinegar, sugar, a little salt (see tips) and pepper. Finally also stir the oil into the dressing. Rinse and shake dry the chives, then cut them into thin rings.

4 Put the breadsticks into a bowl with the radishes, cucumber, celery and alpine cheese. Pour over the dressing and carefully stir to combine. Check and adjust the seasoning of the salad, if necessary, sprinkle with the chives and serve.

USEFUL TIPS

Initially, only add a small amount of salt to the dressing as the breadsticks are salty anyway. It's better to adjust the seasoning at the end.
You also shouldn't leave the salad to stand for too long so that the vegetables and the breadsticks stay nice and crunchy.

OVEN-BAKED POOR KNIGHTS

The classic "Poor Knights" dish asks for day-old bread rolls to be soaked in eggy milk, fried on both sides in clarified butter and finally to be coated in a mixture of sugar and cinnamon. Very tasty indeed! This version is more sophisticated: the "Poor Knights" are baked in the oven and make a great family dish, that's guaranteed!

SWEET AND FRUITY

SERVES 4:
100 g prunes (stoned)
80 g raisins
2 tbsp rum (or apple juice)
80 g sugar
½ tsp ground cinnamon
9 slices stale white tin loaf
(c. 1 cm thick, 300 g, 1–2 days old)
150 g plum purée
650 ml milk
4 eggs (large)
butter for the dish
icing sugar for dusting

HOW LONG IT TAKES: c. 20 min
IN THE OVEN: c. 45 min
PER SERVING: c. 680 kcal | 20 g p | 15 g f | 111 g ch

1 Preheat the oven to 180°C. Cut the prunes into about 1 cm pieces, then put them into a bowl with the raisins and drizzle with the rum. Combine 2 tablespoons of sugar with the cinnamon. Grease an ovenproof dish (c. 18 x 30 cm) with butter.

2 Spread the bread slices with the plum purée and place 3 slices next to each other into the dish. Heat the milk to lukewarm. Reserve 150 ml milk and drizzle the bread slices in the dish with 1 tablespoon of milk each. Cover each slice with 1 tablespoon of the prune and raisin mixture and sprinkle with a little of the cinnamon sugar. Layer the remaining bread slices with the remaining milk and the remaining prune and raisin mixture into the dish as described. Finish with bread slices, laying them with the light, unspread side on top.

3 Using the whisks of a handheld mixer, beat the eggs with the remaining sugar for about 4 minutes until foamy, then slowly stir in the rest of the lukewarm milk. Pour the eggy milk evenly over the bread slices, sprinkle with the remaining cinnamon sugar. Put the dish into the oven (centre, convection 160°C) and bake the Poor Knights for about 45 minutes until golden brown. If the top starts to brown too much, simply cover with baking paper or aluminium foil.

4 Take the dish out of the oven. Leave the Poor Knights to stand briefly, then dust with icing sugar while still hot and serve.

USEFUL TIP

You can turn the Poor Knights into "rich" ones by using the leftovers of a plaited yeast cake or yeast dumplings (p.123) instead of a white loaf. Depending on how sweet you like it, you could also reduce the amount of sugar a little.

LEBKUCHEN SCHMARRN WITH QUINCE

Help! Christmas is gone and we still have lebkuchen! Wrapped into a warm Schmarrn, or torn pancakes, with aromatic spices, they will make many a dessert-lover's heart beat faster.

SOMETHING SPECIAL

SERVES 2:

For the compote:

1 large quince | 1 tbsp sugar
150 ml apple and quince juice (or apple juice)
a dash of lemon juice
1 small piece cinnamon stick | 1 clove

For the Schmarrn:

2 lebkuchen (e.g. with chocolate and/or sugar glaze)
2 tbsp rum (or apple juice)
3 eggs (medium) | 50 g flour
100 ml milk | 2 ½ tbsp cream
1 tsp vanilla sugar (see tip, p.135)
a pinch of salt | 1 tbsp clarified butter
2 tbsp icing sugar
1 ½ tbsp butter
2 tbsp almond flakes
Plus: ovenproof frying pan (28 cm diameter)

HOW LONG IT TAKES: c. 30 min
IN THE OVEN: c. 10 min
PER SERVING: c. 795 kcal | 19 g p | 36 g f | 86 g ch

1 To make the compote, wash the quince, quarter and peel it, remove the core, and cut into about 1 cm wide wedges. In a small saucepan, caramelize the sugar until light brown. Stir in the quince wedges, pour in the apple, quince and lemon juices, and bring to the boil. Add the spices, cover and cook the quince over medium heat for about 10 minutes until soft. Take the saucepan off the stove, leave the compote to cool to lukewarm.

2 Meanwhile, preheat the oven to 180°C (convection is best, or use 200°C top and bottom heat). To make the Schmarrn, cut the lebkuchen into 1 cm pieces and drizzle with the rum. Separate the eggs. Using a whisk, beat the flour, milk, cream, egg yolks and vanilla sugar until you have a smooth batter. Using the whisks of a handheld mixer, beat the egg whites and the salt until stiff, then carefully fold into the batter. Now fold in the lebkuchen pieces.

3 Melt the clarified butter in a frying pan. Spread the batter evenly in the pan and cook on top of the stove over medium heat for about 1 minute. Now put the pan into the oven (centre) and bake for about 10 minutes until golden.

4 Take the pan out of the oven, tip the pancake onto a chopping board and cut into 2 cm pieces. Sprinkle 1 tablespoon icing sugar into the pan and caramelize until light brown. Stir in the butter in small pats. Add the pancake pieces and the almond flakes and caramelize, stirring all the time, for 1–2 minutes to light brown. Dust the lebkuchen Schmarrn with the remaining icing sugar and serve with the quince compote (remove the whole spices).

USEFUL TIP

Schmarrn is also tasty when cooked without the lebkuchen, flavoured with 50 g rum-soaked raisins. If you leave out the gingerbreads, you should whisk the egg whites with 1 tablespoon sugar until stiff.

FESTIVE FEASTS

Christian holidays and traditional festivities are a special time in Bavaria. The girls and boys all dress up to look their best – and things get pretty nice and tasty in the kitchen, too.

WEDDING SOUP WITH THREE GARNISHES

A proper soup is a must – especially for weddings, but also for other festive occasions. With at least three different garnishes the soup will be something special. It's easy: make herb pancakes, semonlina dumplings and liver gnocchi, put them onto the plates and pour over a fine beef broth.

SPECIAL AND TOP FAVOURITE

SERVES 4–6:

For the semolina dumplings (makes about 18):
100 ml milk | 1 tbsp butter
50 g durum wheat semolina | 2 eggs (medium)
soft butter for the dish
pan for baking semolina dumplings (see tips)

For the liver gnocchi (makes 16–18):
1 onion | 2 sprigs marjoram
3 sprigs flat-leaved parsley | 60 g soft butter
fienly grated zest of ½ organic lemon
250 g beef liver (ask the butcher to mince it)
1 egg (medium) | 100 g breadcrumbs
1 tsp beef stock granules (optional)

For the pancakes:
3 tbsp flour | 50 ml milk
1 egg (medium) | 1 sprig flat-leaved parsley
1 small sprig lovage (if liked)
6 chive stems | 1 tsp butter

For the soup:
1–1.5 l beef broth (p.52) | 1 bunch chives

As always:
salt | freshly grated nutmeg
freshly ground black pepper

HOW LONG IT TAKES: c. 10 min (semolina dumplings), c. 20 min (liver gnocchi) and c. 15 min (pancakes)
IN THE OVEN: c. 25 min (semolina dumplings)
IN THE SAUCEPAN: c. 20 min (liver gnocchi)
PER SERVING (when serving 6):
c. 445 kcal | 27 g p | 23 g f | 26 g ch

1 To make the semolina dumplings, bring the milk and butter to the boil in a small saucepan, season with salt and nutmeg. Stir in the semolina and cook for about 2 minutes over medium heat, then transfer to a bowl and leave to cool a little. Stir in the eggs, one at a time, with the whisks of a handheld mixer. Adjust the seasoning with salt and nutmeg.

2 Preheat the oven to 180°C (convection is best, or use 200°C for top and bottom heat). Generously grease the hollows in the pan with butter. Using a teaspoon, divide the semolina mixture between the hollows. Put the pan into the oven (centre) and bake the semolina dumplings for 20–25 minutes until golden. Leave to cool a little then tip out of the pan.

3 To make the liver gnocchi, peel and finely dice the onion. Rinse and shake dry the marjoram and the parsley, pull off and finely chop the leaves. Melt 1 tablespoon of butter in a frying pan, add the onion and sauté for 2 minutes until translucent. Add the herbs and the lemon zest, leave to cool. Beat the remaining butter with a whisk until creamy, stir in first the minced liver and the egg, then the onion mixture and the breadcrumbs. Season with salt, pepper and nutmeg; leave to rise for 10 minutes.

4 In a large, wide saucepan, bring about 2.5 litres water with 1 teaspoon of salt and the beef stock granules, if using, to the boil. Using two tablespoons, shape the liver mixture into gnocchi (16–18 pieces) and let them slide into the boiling water. Always dunk the spoons into the hot water in between so

that the gnocchi slide off the spoons more easily. Bring the water back to the boil. As soon as all the gnocchi have floated to the top, cover the pan with a lid put on at an angle and leave the gnocchi to simmer over low heat for about 20 minutes, then lift out with a slotted spoon.

5 To make the pancakes, put the flour into a bowl and gradually add the milk, whisking constantly. Stir in the egg until you have a smooth, liquid batter. Rinse and shake dry the herbs, pull off and finely chop the leaves of the parsley and the lovage if using, snip the chives into thin rings. Stir the herbs into the batter, season with a little salt and nutmeg and leave to stand for 10 minutes.

6 Melt the butter in a large frying pan (c. 28 cm diameter). Evenly spread the batter, shaking the pan to distribute it, and cook for 1 minute over medium heat. Using a spatula, turn the pancake over and cook the other side for 1 minute. Take the pancake out of the pan and leave to cool. Quarter the pancake so that you get pieces that are roughly the same size. Place the pieces on top of each other, then cut them crossways into thin strips.

7 Bring the beef broth to the boil, adjust the seasoning with salt and pepper. Rinse and shake dry the chives, then snip them into thin rings. Rub a little nutmeg into warm deep plates. Divide the pancake strips, the semonlina dumplings and the liver gnocchi between the plates. Pour over the beef broth, sprinkle with the chives and serve.

USEFUL TIPS

The soup ingredients are easy to prepare ahead and store. Once cooled, arrange the liver gnocchi and the semolina dumplings on a tray and place into the freezer. As soon as the individual dumplings and gnocchi have become firm, they can be transferred to freezer bags or boxes and returned to the freezer. To serve, simply add the frozen dumplings or gnocchi to the boiling hot broth and leave to heat through for 5–10 minutes.

If you like, you can add a pinch of vanilla sugar to the liver mixture for making the gnocchi. The vanilla counters the slightly bitter flavour of the liver.

Special pans are available for making the semolina dumplings (typical in the Danube and Ries area), see the picture above. If you cannot find one, use a cup cake or muffin pan instead.

CRAYFISH SOUP

ELEGANT AND DELICATE

SERVES 6:

1.2 kg crayfish shells (shells from the crayfish dish, p.153)
2 tbsp rapeseed oil | 2 tbsp tomato purée
200 ml red port
2 tbsp brandy
2.5 l root vegetable stock with vegetable strips (p.153)
200 g cream | 2 tbsp cold butter
a pinch of cayenne pepper
salt

HOW LONG IT TAKES: c. 25 min
IN THE SAUCEPAN: c. 1 hour 15 min
PER SERVING: c. 235 kcal | 1 g p | 17 g f | 5 g ch

1 Remove any insides from the shells. Heat the oil in a large, wide saucepan. Add the crayfish shells and fry over high heat for 12–13 minutes. Stir in the tomato purée and fry for 2 minutes, pour in the port and briefly cook to reduce. Add the brandy and light with a long match if liked (to flambé the dish). Pour in the root vegetable stock, bring to the boil and simmer for about 40 minutes over low heat.

2 Using a handheld blender, crush the shells a little, then strain the soup through a sieve, catching the broth and returning it to the saucepan. Bring the crayfish broth to the boil and cook for 30 minutes over medium heat to reduce to 1 litre.

3 Stir in the cream and simmer for about 5 minutes. Mix the butter in small pats into the boiling soup with a blender. Season with cayenne pepper and salt, divide between soup bowls and serve.

USEFUL TIP

If a little crawfish meat is left over from the big crayfish dish (p.153), you can use it to jazz up the soup. Divide the flesh between the soup bowls and pour over the hot soup.

RIVER CRAYFISH IN A VEGETABLE SAUCE

Well, there's not a lot in these tails but goodness, are they tasty! To get the best out of them, you should eat the cooked crayfish with your fingers, nibbling all the goodies inside. The shells, especially, have an intense flavour. Do not throw them away – use them to make a delicious fish soup or a sauce for a pan-fried pike-perch instead.

NOBLE AND FLAVOURSOME

SERVES 2:

1 onion
1 carrot
2 sticks celery
1 leek (c. 70 g)
2 tbsp butter
1½ tsp caraway seeds
150 ml dry white wine
2½ tsp salt
2 large sprigs dill (without the tips!)
40 live crayfish (1.8–2 kg)
baguette, to serve

HOW LONG IT TAKES: c. 25 min
PER SERVING: c. 670 kcal | 68 g p | 11 g f | 62 g ch

1 Peel and halve the onion, then cut it into thin strips. Wash or peel the vegetables, then cut them into thin, 5-cm-long strips.

2 Melt the butter in a wide, tall saucepan. Add the onion and vegetables and fry for 2 minutes until translucent. Add the caraway seeds and stir, pour in the white wine and bring to the boil. Add 4 litres boiling hot water and season with the salt. Rinse the dill and add it to the boiling stock.

3 Now put the living crayfish head-first into the stock, cover, bring to the boil, then take off the stove and leave to cook for 6–8 minutes in the residual heat. The cooking time may vary depending on the size of the crayfish, so make sure you lift a crayfish out of the stock early on, separate the tail from the head and break open the shell. The crayfish tails are perfect when they have a glossy shimmer. They shoud not be cooked for too long because the crayfish flesh will dry out.

4 Arrange the crayfish in a larger soup dish, pour over a little of the root vegetable stock and the vegetable strips and serve with baguette slices. To eat the crayfish, separate the claws from the body, carefully pull apart the claws and remove the shells. Using the back of a knife, hit and crack the thicker parts of the claws, break the shells apart and separate out the flesh. Twist the head off the tail, squeeze the tail shells together and break them open, remove the flesh.

USEFUL TIPS

As the crayfish are to be broken open and eaten with your fingers, place a finger bowl (a bowl with lukewarm water and a few lemon wedges) on the table. This allows you to clean your fingers during and after the meal. If you have ordered crayfish in a restaurant it's possible that you will be issued with a bib to protect your clothes – at times liquid squirts from the shells as you are breaking them open. A large napkin or a cloth will also do.
In the shops you can find special lobster-eating utensils, which certainly make it easier to get to the delicious crayfish flesh. So, if you often eat crayfish, it would be a worthwhile purchase.

SWEETBREADS WITH ASPARAGUS AND MORELS

An amazing dish with three main ingredients that harmonize perfectly. Somehow nature is just too clever – it delivers us foods that go well together all at the same time.

FOR BAVARIAN GOURMETS
SERVES 2:
2 veal sweetbreads (c. 250 g each)
10 g dried morels
500 g white asparagus
1 onion | 3 tbsp butter
a pinch of sugar | 50 ml dry white wine
50 ml vegetable stock | 150 g cream
salt | freshly ground black pepper
1 tsp clarified butter
½ bunch chives

HOW LONG IT TAKES: c. 1 hour
PER SERVING: c. 1100 kcal | 33 g p | 102 g f | 9 g ch

1 Trim the sweetbreads by removing all the sinews, membranes and any remaining veins. Put the sweetbreads into cold water and leave them to soak for about 30 minutes, changing the water several times. Put the morels into lukewarm water and soak for about 20 minutes. Take the sweetbreads out of the water, pat dry with kitchen paper and cut each into 2 equal pieces. Strain the morels, squeeze out, drain on kitchen paper and halve or quarter depending on their size.

2 Meanwhile, peel the asparagus and cut off the woody ends. Divide each spear into 3 even-sized pieces. Peel and very finely dice the onion.

3 In a frying pan, melt 2 tablespoons of butter. Sprinkle in the sugar and stir briefly, add the asparagus and fry for 5–6 minutes over medium heat until pale. Add the morels and fry for 1 minute. Pour in the white wine and the vegetable stock, cover and simmer over low heat for 1–2 minutes. Stir in the cream, cover again with the lid, simmer for another 3 minutes. Season with salt and pepper.

4 Meanwhile, melt the clarified butter in a second large frying pan. Add the sweetbread pieces and fry over medium heat. Season with salt and pepper and fry another 1 minute, then turn. Careful – they may spit! Push the sweetbread pieces to the side of the pan, add the onion dice and fry for 1 minute. Add the remaining butter and cook the sweetbreads for about 7 minutes over low heat, turning the onion and the sweetbreads occasionally. Then cover and cook for another 5 minutes until done.

5 Rinse and shake dry the chives, then cut them into thin rings. Take the sweetbreads out of the pan and leave to rest, then cut into 1½ cm wide slices. Arrange the sweetbreads with the onion, asparagus and morels on plates, sprinkle with chives and serve. This is good with sautéed potatoes.

USEFUL TIP

During the tradition morel season – March/April/May – it is best to use fresh and not dried morels. Use 3–5 morels per person, depending on their size. Thoroughly trim the morels, rinse under running water if necessary, as dirt often collects in their pits. Halve or quarter the morels depending on size and cook as described above.

PARTYTIME IN BAVARIA

A RICHTIGA KIRTA DAUAD BIS ZUM IRDA.
ES KO SE AA SCHICKA BIS ZUM MIGGA.
UND KON DE BEIRIN GUAD KOCHA,
DAUAD A DE GANZE WOCHA.
Which translates roughly as:
A true parish fair lasts 'til Tuesday.
But can even go to Wednesday.
And if the farmer's wife is a good cook,
it will run the entire week.

Many international visitors, especially those from further afield, consider Bavarian traditions, with armfuls of massive beer steins served by pretty girls in low-cut dirndl dresses, and strapping lederhosen-clad men blowing alpine horns, the epitome of the German lifestyle. At the time of the kingdom's founding in 1806, Bavaria had precious little in common with the other German territories. The fact that the Napoleonic land reforms saw Bavarians ultimately melded with Franks, Swabians and Palatines, despite their differing cultural roots, made for a predictably difficult start. Over the centuries, however, the inhabitants of this beautiful land became instilled with distinct way of life and fortitude and individuality. And even to this day, Bavarians remain passionnate about fostering and passing on to future generations their uniqueness and customs.

The rural cycle of work and religious holidays has many occasions where Bavarians can celebrate their traditions. All provide a colourful array of traditional, church, village and forest festivals and processions in local costumes, with brass music, abundant beer-drinking and hearty food. There's the driving down of cattle from mountain pastures, the Gäuboden folk festival, the Georgiritt horse-back procession, the Leonhardi horse-carriage procession, the raising of the maypole, parish fairs, harvest thanksgiving, the Perchten parade with its scary masks and many more.

SIT DOWN, ...

... together we are more. Nowhere else are traditions preserved as intensively as in the Bavarian marksmen's clubs. To protect the country from "wilful invasion and harm", citizens and farmers in the early 1500s were examined and grouped into powerful, solid defence teams. The marksmen continue to symbolise the willingness "to defend Bavarian folk culture" to this day.

Worship of the Virgin Mary is closely entwined with this shooting tradition, as the Mother of Jesus is the patron saint of the "Gebirgsschützen" (Mountain Guards). For this reason, almost every village in Bavaria today still has a marksmen's club, with its corresponding annual "Schützenfest" – a festival combined with church service and street procession.

Even the most famous costume worn on all special occasions – lederhosen for men and a colourful corset for women – can be traced back to Upper Bavarian alpine dress. The "Gamsbart" (the tuft of chamois hair on the hats), which can end up costing several hundred pounds, is an essential touch as an authentic hat adornment.

Costumes can vary greatly depending on region, but any modern variations with trainers, inappropriate shirts or improper skirt lengths are widely frowned upon as abominations. After all, a costume, according to the express wishes of the House of Wittelsbach, should help to "strengthen Bavarian patriotism" and boost confidence vis-à-vis the Prussians. The costumes reach amusing, at times shocking, new lows every year at Munich's Oktoberfest, where people from all over the world celebrate all things Bavarian, wearing what they believe to be traditional garb.

OH, WE DO LIKE TO BE BESIDE THE LAKESIDE

Lakes feature just as much in the idyllic notion of the Upper Bavarian alpine foothills as dirndl dresses, lederhosen, beer steins and bread dumplings. And nowadays, many people live as luxuriously and sumptuously on Bavarian lakeshores as they do on Miami Beach, but less dangerously.

It was by the lakeside that, on 24 August in years gone by, the feast day of St Bartholomew, the patron saint of fishermen, was established. The day marks the end of the close and spawning seasons on Bavaria's lakes and rivers, and this is celebrated with a festival for the Fisher King and his best catch, as well as the "Fischerstechen", a water jousting competition. This exhilarating game sees grown men try and knock each other off their boats using long poles.

Bavaria's lake district stretches from the Allgäu region almost as far as greater Salzburg, but in fact starts at Lake Constance, whose eastern end is firmly entrenched in Bavarian territory. Lake Ammersee lies next to three smaller bodies of water known as the Wesslinger See, Wörthsee and Pilsensee in the "Fünf-Seen-Land" or Five Lakes District southwest of Munich. Rising up on the eastern shores of this scenic gem is the "Heiliger Berg" (Holy Mountain), with the Andechs Benedictine abbey and its famous brewery. The fifth lake in this cluster is the most popular and easily accessible bathing lake for Munich locals. The shores of Lake Starnberg are lined with castles and manors, boasting vast gardens and private footbridges for the rich and beautiful.

Further afield is Tegernsee which – despite being another haunt of the smart set – has managed to preserve much of its natural beauty. It is the ideal place for tourists pushed for time, as Tegernsee Abbey condenses "all of Bavaria" under one roof, as historian Heinrich von Treitschke once noted: a ducal palace, a former abbey church and the inevitable brewery.

Finally, shimmering magnificently in the foothills of the Alps, is the lake Staffelsee, situated in the Murnauer Moos marshlands, which is known to attract many prominent artists. To the east lie Walchensee and Kochelsee, lakes which King Maximilian of Bavaria considered to be "the finest part of my kingdom". The Chiemgau region in Bavaria's southeast is home to several more lakes, the largest of which being Chiemsee, the "Bavarian Sea".

But Bavaria's fish are just as noteworthy as its lakes. In addition to common brown and rainbow trout, grayling, pike, pike-perch, ruffe, vimba bream, roach and rudd, other edible fish include:

WHITEFISH: A flavoursome fish which tastes delicious when freshly grilled fish on a stick, and is also known as the "Bavarian fishermen's breadwinner".

BROWN TROUT (LAKE-DWELLING): The silvery salmonid found in Upper Bavaria can grow to lengths of around 1.4 metres, and weigh up to 30 kilograms.

RUTILUS MEIDINGERI (PEARL FISH): A ray-finned species unique to Lake Chiemsee, and one of Germany's rarest fish.

DEEPWATER CHAR: This special type of char is only found in the lakes Königsee and Ammersee.

CATFISH WITH THREE TYPES OF MUSTARD

You'll be thrilled to discover that frying brings out the best in a catfish. Plus spices normally used for pickling add a special touch to this exceptionally aromatic sauce.

DOWN TO EARTH AND TANGY

SERVES 4:

700 g fillet of wels catfish (without skin)
1 leek (white parts, c. 80 g)
3 button mushrooms
1 tbsp marinated pot roast spice mix (see tips, p.176)
2 tbsp butter
2 tbsp flour
100 ml dry white wine
400 ml fish stock (from a jar)
200 g cream
salt | freshly ground black pepper
2 pinches of sugar
juice of ½ lemon
1 heaped tbsp clarified butter
3 sprigs dill
1 tsp each hot, medium-hot and Bavarian sweet mustard
Plus: paper teabag

HOW LONG IT TAKES: c. 45 min
PER SERVING: c. 560 kcal | 30 g p | 42 g f | 9 g ch

1 Remove any remaining bones from the catfish fillet, cut the fillet into pieces weighing 80–90 g each. Trim, wash and finely dice the leek. Clean the mushrooms and chop into smaller pieces if necessary. Put the pot roast spice mix into a teabag, close tightly.

2 Melt the butter in a saucepan. Add the leek and fry for about 2 minutes. Add the mushrooms and fry for 1 minute. Dust both with 1 tablespoon of flour and fry for 1 minute, stirring constantly, then gradually stir in the wine and the stock. Place the spice bag into the sauce and simmer for about 5 minutes over low heat. Take out and discard the spice bag. Pour the cream into the sauce and simmer for 9–10 minutes to reduce to a velvety consistency.

3 Meanwhile, season the catfish pieces with salt, pepper, sugar and lemon juice, then dust on both sides with the remaining flour. Melt the clarified butter in a large frying pan. Add the fish fillets and fry over high heat for 3 minutes, turn, then cook over low heat for 8–10 minutes.

4 Rinse and shake dry the dill, pull off and finely chop the tips. Stir the three types of mustard into the sauce, adjust the seasoning with salt and pepper, and finely purée with a handheld blender. Flavour the sauce with the dill and arrange on plates with the catfish. Kohlrabi steamed in butter and boiled potatoes would make a perfect accompaniment.

GOOD WITH: STEAMED KOHLRABI

Peel 800 g kohlrabi, place some of the nicer leaves into cold water. Cut the kohlrabi bulb into 1-cm-wide and 6-cm-long sticks. Melt 2 tablespoons of butter in a wide saucepan, add the kohlrabi and sauté briefly. Pour in 150 ml water or vegetable stock, season with a pinch of salt. Cover and steam the kohlrabi for about 10 minutes over low heat until soft, turning it occasionally. Rinse and shake dry 3–4 sprigs parsley, pull off the leaves and roughly chop and sprinkle over the kohlrabi leaves, then add both to the steamed kohlrabi. Season with salt and freshly grated nutmeg to taste.

PIKE-PERCH WITH CEPS AND JERUSALEM ARTICHOKES

For a long time, Jerusalem artichokes were sidelined by the potato. Nowadays, however, they have become fashionable once more, even with gourmets, because they are very versatile. They can be enjoyed, for example, as a purée, raw or even as crisps.

EXTRAVAGANT AND DELICATE
SERVES 4:
For the purée:
600 g Jerusalem artichokes
salt | 1½ tbsp butter
For the mushrooms:
300 g ceps
1 onion | 1 small garlic clove
3 sprigs flat-leaved parsley
2 tbsp butter
salt | freshly ground black pepper
freshly grated nutmeg
For the sauce:
80 g cold butter | 1 egg yolk (large)
2 tbsp dry white wine
salt | freshly ground black pepper
freshly grated nutmeg
For the fish:
4 pike-perch fillets (with skin, c. 120 g each)
2 tbsp vegetable oil | salt

HOW LONG IT TAKES: c. 50 min
PER SERVING: c. 435 kcal | 29 g p | 32 g f | 6 g ch

1 To make the purée, wash, peel and roughly chop the Jerusalem artichokes, bring to the boil in salted water and cook for about 20 minutes until done. Drain, return to the stove and cook over low heat for 5 minutes. Mash with a potato masher and stir in the butter. Cover and keep warm in a water bath.

2 Meanwhile, clean the ceps and cut into about ½ cm pieces. Peel and finely dice the onion and the garlic. Rinse and shake dry the parsley, pull off and roughly chop the leaves. Heat 1 tablespoon of butter in a frying pan. Add the ceps, season with salt and fry over high heat for 2 minutes. Add the onion, garlic and the remaining butter, continue frying the mushrooms for 4 minutes until golden. Stir in the parsley, season with salt, pepper and nutmeg. Set aside.

3 To make the sauce, melt the butter. In a metal bowl, stir together the egg yolk with the wine and 2 tablespoons of water. Season with salt, pepper and nutmeg. Over a hot waterbath, beat the sauce with a whisk for 3 minutes until frothy, take off the stove and gradually stir in the butter. Set aside.

4 Remove any remaining fish bones, cut slashes into the fillet skins. Heat the oil in a large frying pan. Salt the pike-perch and place skin side down in the hot fat. Fry over medium heat for about 3 minutes until crisp, turn, fry briefly. Take the pan off the stove and leave fillets to cook for 2–3 minutes in the residual heat. Preheat the oven grill.

5 Meanwhile put the purée in the middle of ovenproof plates. Add the ceps and the sauce. Put the plates in the top of the oven, one at a time and grill everything for 3 minutes until golden brown. Take out, place the fish on top and serve.

CHAR WITH ONION AND SPINACH

After the trout, the char is probably the Bavarians' favourite freshwater fish. The tender fillets are quickly cooked and are a dream fried with their skins. Leave very fresh fillets to rest in the fridge for a day, or else they will roll up when frying.

DOWN TO EARTH AND GOOD

SERVES 4:

For the spinach:

1.2 kg fresh spinach leaves | 1 large onion
1 large garlic clove
3 tbsp cold butter | 200 g cream
salt | freshly ground black pepper
freshly grated nutmeg

For the fish:

8 char fillets (with skins, c. 100 g each)
salt | freshly ground black pepper
2 tbsp flour | 2 tbsp clarified butter
2 tsp butter

HOW LONG IT TAKES: c. 45 min
PER SERVING: c. 525 kcal | 46 g p | 34 g f | 8 g ch

1 Thoroughly clean the spinach leaves and remove the stalks. If necessary, wash the spinach several times and drain thoroughly. Peel and finely dice the onion and the garlic. Remove any remaining bones from the char fillets. In a kettle, bring plenty of water to the boil.

2 To cook the spinach, melt 2 tablespoons of butter in a wide saucepan. Add the onion and the garlic, fry over medium heat for about 5 minutes. Pour in the cream, bring to the boil and cook for 2 minutes.

3 Meanwhile, put half the spinach into a large sieve, put it into the sink and pour over boiling water to make the leaves collapse. Carefully squeeze out the spinach and add it the the cream sauce. Do the same with the rest of the spinach. Bring everything to the boil, season with salt, pepper and nutmeg, and simmer for 4 minutes over low heat. Stir the remaining butter into the spinach in small pats, leave to simmer for 1 minute, then take off the stove.

4 Season the fish fillets on both sides with salt and pepper, then dust with flour. Melt the clarified butter in two large frying pans. Place the fish fillets skinside down and fry over high heat for about 3 minutes, turn and fry for another 1 minute. Put 1 teaspoon of butter into each pan, drizzle the fish fillets with the frying juices, take the pans off the stove, leave the fillets to cook in the residual heat for 1 minute until juicy.

5 Bring the spinach to the boil again and arrange on plates with the crisply fried char, serve. Good side dishes are potatoes boiled in their skins and turned in butter, or potato pancakes.

GOOD WITH: POTATO PANCAKES

Peel and coarsely grate 1 kg waxy potatoes boiled until al dente. Season with salt, pepper and nutmeg. In a small frying pan, melt 1 tablespoon of clarified butter. Arrange a quarter of the potatoes flat in the pan and fry over medium heat for 3 minutes, then turn carefully. Add a little more butter, fry the other side for 3 minutes. Turn again and fry for another 2 minutes. Drain the potato pancake on kitchen paper and keep warm on a baking tray in the oven at 120°C. Prepare the remaining three quarters of potatoes in the same way.

Ehrentisch
Ehrentisch

SUCKLING PIG WITH HOPS AND MALT

The tender leg of suckling pig cooks in the oven in a sauce of vegetables, meat stock and malt beer, and it is the sweetish malt beer which gives this little piglet its delicious flavour.

JUICY AND CRISPY

SERVES 4–6:

1.8 kg leg of suckling pig (without central and hip bones, ask the butcher to remove them and to chop 400 g bones)
600 g pork spareribs (ask the butcher to cut them into small pieces)
2 onions
1 carrot
1 piece celeriac (c. 200 g)
1½ garlic cloves
1 tbsp vegetable oil | 1 tbsp flour
1.6 l meat stock (from a jar, or water)
¼ l malt beer
salt | freshly ground black pepper
4 pinches of ground caraway seeds
2 tsp cornflour
Plus: kitchen twine

HOW LONG IT TAKES: c. 45 min
IN THE OVEN: c. 2 hours 50 min
PER SERVING (when serving 6):
c. 615 kcal | 58 g p | 36 g f | 10 g ch

1 Preheat the oven to 200°C (convection is best, or use 220°C top and bottom heat). Briefly wash and pat dry the bones of the suckling pig leg and the spareribs, then place them onto a baking tray. Put into the oven (centre) and roast for about 30 minutes until golden brown, then take out. Lower the oven temperature to 150°C (convection, 170°C top and bottom heat). Peel the onions, carrot and celeriac and cut everything into 1 cm cubes. Peel the garlic and finely dice 1 of the cloves.

2 Heat the oil in a roasting pan (c. 25 x 35 cm). Add the onions and the vegetables and fry over medium heat for 7–8 minutes. Add the bones, cook for 1 minute. Dust everything with flour, fry for another 1 minute. Add a dash of the meat stock and cook to reduce. Repeat twice. Pour in the remaining meat stock and 200 ml malt beer, and bring to the boil.

3 Season the leg on the meat side with salt, pepper, 2 pinches of caraway seeds and the diced garlic, then tie up with kitchen twine. Place the leg, skin side down, into the pan and cook in the oven (centre) for 1 hour 30 minutes. Turn the leg over and cook for another 40 minutes until tender. Take out the pan and remove the meat. Turn the oven to the grill function (top level). Slice the remaining garlic.

4 Strain the contents of the pan through a sieve, catching the juices in a saucepan, bring to the boil. Stir together the cornflour with 2–3 tablespoons of cold water. Stir the remaining malt beer and the slices of garlic into the sauce, then cook for 15–20 minutes over medium heat until velvety. Season with salt, pepper and the remaining caraway seeds.

5 In a cup, stir ½ teaspoon of salt into about 100 ml water. Place the pork leg onto a grid and put into the oven (centre), place a baking tray as drip guard underneath. Brush the leg with the salt water and grill for about 10 minutes until crisp, brushing repeatedly with salt water. Take the finished roast out of the oven, remove the kitchen twine, carve the leg and serve with the sauce. The pork is particularly good with potato or bread dumplings (p.88/89).

A REALLY GOOD BEEF POT ROAST

For this, the quality of the meat is of vital importance. You will only get a juicy pot roast with a delicious sauce if you use a well-hung shoulder of beef. Go to a butcher you can trust.

JUICY ... AND WHAT A SAUCE

SERVES 4:

2 onions | 1 carrot
1 piece celeriac (c. 100 g)
1.3 kg boneless shoulder roast of beef
salt | freshly ground black pepper
2 generous pinches of flour
3 tbsp vegetable oil | 2 tbsp tomato purée
1 tsp brown sugar
½ l full-bodied red wine (e.g. Cabernet Sauvignon)
1 l beef broth (p.52, or meat stock from a jar)
1 piece of gingerbread (c. 50 g)
6 parsley stems (without the leaves!)
1 tsp juniper berries | 3 cloves
1 tsp black peppercorns
1 tsp allspice berries | 3 bay leaves
1–2 tsp cornflour (depending on the desired sauce consistency)

HOW LONG IT TAKES: c. 45 min
IM TOPF: c. 3 hours
PER SERVING: c. 950 kcal | 75 g p | 53 g f | 17 g ch

1 Peel the onions, carrot and celeriac and cut into in 1½ cm dice. Cut away any sinews from the beef if necessary, then season all over with salt and pepper and dust with flour.

2 Heat the oil in a casserole dish. Add the meat and fry over high heat for 2 minutes, turn and fry for another 2 minutes. Now “stand” the meat on its end and also fry the sides of the roast for about another 2 minutes. Take the meat out of the casserole and transfer it to a plate.

3 Put the onions and the vegetables into the casserole and fry for about 5 minutes until light brown. Stir in the tomato purée, sprinkle with sugar and fry for 2 minutes. Add a dash of red wine and cook for 2 minutes to reduce, then add another dash of wine and cook for about 3 minutes to reduce. Repeat this process twice. Add the remaining red wine and the beef broth, return the meat to the casserole and bring to the boil again. Roughly chop the gingerbread and add to the casserole. Cover the roast and cook over a low heat for about 2 hours, turning it over from time to time.

4 Rinse and shake dry the parsley, add to the sauce together with the spices and the bay leaves. Leave the roast to braise for another 1 hour until it is done. It should be beautifully tender when pricked with a fork, which should easily come out of the flesh.

5 Lift the cooked pot roast out of the sauce and set aside. Strain the sauce through a fine sieve, catching the liquid. Press the vegetables and aromatics through the sieve, discard the remains. Return sauce and meat to the casserole and bring to the boil. Stir the cornflour into 2–3 tablespoons of cold water (use more or less cornflour depending on the desired consistency of the sauce), stir it into the sauce and simmer to reduce over medium heat for 5 minutes until velvety. Adjust the seasoning.

6 Cut the beef pot roast into just under finger-thick slices and arrange on warm plates. Top with the sauce and serve. A great accompaniment would be the homemade spaetzle (p.93).

OX CHEEKS WITH WATERCRESS

Ox cheeks are delicious not only when braised but also when boiled. The muscular, marbled meat has a very special flavour.

UNUSUAL AND SLIGHTLY HOT

SERVES 4:

4 ox cheeks (c. 370 g each, pre-order from the butcher)
salt | freshly ground black pepper
2 tbsp vegetable oil
1 onion | 1 carrot
1 leek (c. 80 g) | 1 large tomato
1 piece celeriac (c. 250 g)
1 parsley root
1 garlic clove
1 tsp black peppercorns
1 tsp juniper berries
1 tsp allspice berries | 2 bay leaves
2 tbsp butter | 1 bunch watercress
200 g cream
½ tsp horseradish (from a jar)
Plus: kitchen twine

HOW LONG IT TAKES: c. 35 min
IN THE SAUCEPAN: c. 3 hours 45 min
PER SERVING: c. 2265 kcal | 40 g p | 231 g f | 7 g ch

1 In a tall saucepan, bring 3.5 litres water to the boil. Free the ox cheeks from any sinews if necessary, then tie them into little parcels with the kitchen twine. Season with salt and pepper. Heat the oil in a frying pan. Add the cheeks and fry for 2 minutes, then fry for another 1 minute all over, turning them. Put them into the boiling water and cook over high heat for 6–8 minutes. Using a slotted spoon, frequently lift off the scum that forms on top. Reduce the temperature and cook the ox cheeks over medium heat for 1 hour.

2 Wash and halve the onion, place cut side down into a frying pan and fry over medium heat for about 4–5 minutes until dark. Peel or wash and trim the vegetables. Halve the carrot and the leek, quarter the tomato. Cut a third of the celeriac and the parsley root into 1 cm dice, halve the remaining celeriac piece. Crush the garlic clove in its skin.

3 Put the onion, carrot, leek, tomato, celeriac half, garlic, spices and bay leaves into the saucepan. Gently simmer the cheeks for another 2 hours 45 minutes over low heat until cooked. Cooking time may vary according to the quality of the meat. Test regularly whether the meat is done – a meat fork stuck into the meat should easily come out again.

4 Some 45 minutes before the end of the cooking time, ladle off 350 ml meat broth and strain through a sieve. Melt 1 tablespoon of butter in a small, tall saucepan. Add the remaining vegetable cubes and fry for 2 minutes, then pour in 200 ml of the broth, bring to the boil, cover and simmer over low heat for about 30 minutes. Wash the cress, remove the stems and shake dry; reserve a few leaves. Finely purée the vegetables in the saucepan with a handheld blender. Pour in the cream and the remaining broth, bring to the boil, stir in the remaining butter and the water-cress. Season with salt, pepper and horseradish.

5 Take the cooked ox cheeks out of the saucepan, remove the twine. Slice the meat and arrange on hot plates with the sauce, lightly salt the cheeks. Garnish with the reserved cress leaves and serve. Delicious with freshly grated horseradish.

OUR FABLED KING

The Bavarians were not overly fond of their "Kini", King Ludwig II, when he was alive; after all, his hobby castles cost a fortune, and he barely bothered about politics or the common people. Today, on the other hand, even the most conservative of Gamsbart-wearers indulgently glorify him as a nostalgic icon. He has become the fairytale king, who embodies the "good old days". And in hindsight, he has somehow managed to make a positive contribution, for Bavarian tourism doesn't do too badly out of his array of royal fairytale castles.

The monarch withdrew early from public life, at the tender age of thirty, focusing solely on his architectural visions: his Herrenchiemsee Palace was intended to outdo Versailles, but was never completed – perhaps due to the excessive scale of the plan. Linderhof Palace in the Ammergau Alps was completed, and it was here that the romanticist spent a lot of his spare time venerating the composer Richard Wagner. The king even had one of his favourite footmen row him around the Venus Grotto (an artificially created dripstone cave) in a shell-like gondola wearing a costume of one of Wagner's romantic operas, Lohengrin. In the 19th century, one of the first electric lights was used to illuminate this grotto, and in a great variety of colours to boot.

And speaking of technology: King Ludwig's passion for gadgets, which he used to modernise his magic dream castles, ultimately led to him being declared certified insane. This wasn't based on Bavaria's very first telephone at Neuschwanstein, or on the central heating system he had installed there, or even on the automatic toilet flushes. Nor was it based on the battery-powered moon shining above the elaborate royal sleighs on which "Mad" King Ludwig would often glide like a vision through the snow at night. The real peak of all his eccentric endeavours was most likely his plan for a flying cable car powered by steam engines and decorated like a peacock, designed to enable the king to hover over the alpine lake.

Declared incompetent, lonely and deeply worried about the completion of his constructions, the "Kini" mysteriously died in Lake Starnberg.

Today, mementos of him can be found in every souvenir shop, on beer steins and snuffboxes, and anything else tourists believe to be typically Bavarian.

However, fans of the Bavarian monarchy, in their cult following of the "Kini", actually mourn a member of the House of Wittelsbach who was not a king at all: Prince Regent Luitpold ran state affairs for a quarter of a century, distributed cigars to the people, and was an avid hunter. His grandfather, King Maximilian I, enjoyed similar popularity. The Bavarians' relationship with their kings was nevertheless always ambiguous, characterized by a certain penchant for boldness and fanfare. While the last monarch, King Ludwig III, looked somewhat like Luitpold, he was a boring king, and paid for this by being exiled in 1918. Then again, there was another ruler who was also sent packing by the Bavarians, despite him being far from boring: King Ludwig I, though he at least left behind a "Gallery of Beauties", a collection of portraits.

SOUR AND SPICY VEAL TAILS

Real Bavarians enjoy the authentic, traditional and correct way of eating veal tails: picking them up with their hands and nibbling the meat off the bones with their teeth.

TASTY AND DOWN TO EARTH

SERVES 4–6:

1 carrot | 1 leek (c. 120 g)
1 piece celeriac (c. 140 g)
1 large onion
24–26 pieces of veal tail (c. 2.5 kg, from the butcher)
salt | freshly ground black pepper
2 tbsp flour | 4 tbsp vegetable oil
2 tbsp tomato purée
½ l rosé wine
1.6 l meat stock or veal stock (from a jar)
2 tbsp marinated pot roast spice mix (see tips)
3 sage leaves | 1 tsp brown sugar

HOW LONG IT TAKES: c. 1 hour
IN THE SAUCEPAN: c. 2 hours
PER SERVING (when serving 6):
c. 320 kcal | 26 g p | 13 g f | 13 g ch

1 Peel or wash and trim the vegetables and cut them into 1 cm cubes. Peel and finely dice the onion. Season the veal tails with salt and pepper and dust all over with flour.

2 Heat the oil in a wide saucepan. Add the veal tails and dust with the remaining flour. Fry the meat for 5 minutes over high heat, turn and fry for another 5 minutes. Take out of the saucepan. Put the vegetables (but not the leek) and the onion into the saucepan and fry for 3 minutes, stirring constantly. Stir in the tomato purée and fry for 2 minutes. Add a dash of rosé wine and cook for 5 minutes to reduce, then add a little more and cook for another 5 minutes to reduce. Pour in the remaining wine and the stock, add the veal tails, sprinkle in the marinated pot roast spice mix and bring everything to the boil. Cover and braise over a low heat for about 2 hours until the meat is tender, turning the veal tails occasionally during cooking.

3 Take the cooked veal tails out of the saucepan. Strain the sauce through a fine sieve, catching the liquid, then return to the pan. Bring the sauce to the boil and cook over medium heat for about 12 minutes to reduce. Cut the sage leaves into thin strips and add to the sauce with the leek, then season with the sugar. Return the veal tails to the saucepan and braise for another 6–7 minutes over low heat. Check and adjust the seaoning with salt and pepper.

4 Arrange the veal tails with their bones and plenty of sauce in deep plates. Particularly delicious when enjoyed with wide ribbon pasta, boiled potatoes or bread dumplings (p.89).

USEFUL TIPS

Marinated pot roast spice mix is a colourful mix of dried vegetables, herbs and spices. The most commonly found ingredients are bay leaves, juniper berries, allspice berries, mustard seeds and black peppercorns as well as dried cubes of celeriac, garlic, carrots and dried parsley. Mix your own if you cannot find it in a supermarket.

If you prefer you could of course serve the braised veal tails off the bone. Simply separate the meat from the bones and heat through in the sauce. Any leftovers can be preserved: bring to the boil, transfer to clean jars, close, leave to cool, then chill.

POT-ROAST BELLY OF VEAL WITH KIDNEY STUFFING

This stuffed veal roast is a classic Sunday dish. Cleaned and trimmed kidney chunks are rolled in a piece of veal belly and tied as a pot roast with kitchen twine.

A BAVARIAN ORIGINAL

SERVES 4:

1 carrot
1 piece celeriac (c. 150 g) | 1 large onion
400 g veal bones (chopped by the butcher)
1.3 kg belly of veal stuffed with kidneys (must be pre-ordered from the butcher!)
salt | freshly ground black pepper
2 tbsp vegetable oil | 2 tbsp tomato purée
800 ml meat stock or veal stock (from a jar, or water)
1 tbsp marinated pot roast spice mix (see tips, p.176)
1 sprig tarragon
1 tsp cornflour
Plus: kitchen twine

HOW LONG IT TAKES: c. 30 min
IN THE OVEN: c. 2 hours 45 min
PER SERVING: c. 525 kcal | 56 g p | 29 g f | 10 g ch

1 Preheat the oven to 160° C. Peel the carrot, celeriac and onion, then cut into 1 cm dice. Wash and drain the bones. Tie the roast lengthways with twine (see tip), season with salt and pepper.

2 Heat the oil in a roasting pan with a lid. Add the veal joint and fry for 1 minute, then fry the other sides, turning, for about 2–3 minutes. Take the meat out of the pan. Put in the bones and fry for 3 minutes over medium heat. Add the onion and the vegetables and fry everything for another 3 minutes. Add the tomato purée and fry for 3 minutes, stirring. Pour in 100 ml stock, cook for 1 minute to reduce. Add the remaining stock, bring to the boil, sprinkle in the spice mix. Add the meat, cover and cook in the oven (centre, convection 140°C) for 45 minutes. Turn the roast over and cook for another 1 hour 45 minutes, turning a few times after 1 hour. Finally take off the lid and cook uncovered for 15 minutes, so that the roast will be nicely browned on top.

3 Take the roaster out of the oven, remove the meat. Strain the sauce into a saucepan through a fine sieve, bring to the boil. Rinse the tarragon and add to the sauce, cook over medium heat for 5 minutes to reduce. Combine the cornflour with 2–3 tablespoons of cold water, stir into the sauce, cook for 5 minutes until velvety. Season with salt and plenty of pepper.

4 Remove the twine from the pot roast, then cut it into finger-thick slices. Arrange the slices on hot plates with the sauce. Serve with bread dumplings (p.89), potato purée (p.95), spaetzle or finger gnocchi (p.93). Also delicious with fried button mushrooms or chanterelles and a green salad.

USEFUL TIP

Although the butcher will have tied the veal pot roast with the veal stuffing inside, it's best to additionally tie it lengthways with twine so that none of the delicious stuffing falls out during cooking and the frequent turning in the roasting pan.

ST MARTIN'S GOOSE

The season for slaughtering geese begins on November 11, St Martin's Day. And so in Bavaria a crisply roasted goose is a must on St Martin's Day, at Christmas and of course every church's patron saint day.

CRISP OUTSIDE, JUICY INSIDE

SERVES 5–6:

For the goose and stuffing:

1 goose (c. 4.7 kg)
2 large onions
2 tart apples (e.g. Boskoop)
1 slice brown bread
2 sprigs dried mugwort (optional)
½ tsp black peppercorns | salt
2 bay leaves
½ tsp caraway seeds
a few wooden toothpicks or kitchen twine and needle

For the sauce:

700 g goose bones (pre-order from your poultry butcher and ask for the bones to be chopped)
3 onions | 1 carrot
1 piece celeriac (c. 150 g)
2 tbsp vegetable oil | 2 tbsp tomato purée
300 ml full-bodied red wine (e.g. Cabernet Sauvignon)
1 heaped tbsp flour
1 l goose stock or meat stock (from a jar)
2 bay leaves
1 tsp black peppercorns
½ tsp juniper berries
½ tsp allspice berries
1 sprig dried mugwort (if liked)
1 piece zest of an organic orange (6–8 cm)
salt

HOW LONG IT TAKES: c. 1 hour
IN THE OVEN: c. 4 hours 30 min
PER SERVING (when serving 6):
c. 2090 kcal | 92 g p | 181 g f | 14 g ch

1 Preheat the oven to 200°C (convection is best, or 220°C top and bottom heat). If necessary, remove the offal from the goose's belly cavity. Pat dry with kitchen paper. Remove the belly fat and set aside. (The offal can be used as described in the tips on p.185 if liked.) Cut off and roughly chop the wing bones and the neck.

2 To make the sauce, put the goose bones, the wing bones and the neck on a baking tray and roast in the oven (centre) for about 30 minutes until golden brown, turning the bones several times. Take the tray out of the oven and add 200 ml water to loosen the cooking juices, then set aside. Reduce the oven temperature to 120°C (convection, 140°C top and bottom heat).

3 Meanwhile, make the stuffing. Peel and roughly dice the onions. Wash and quarter the apples and remove the cores, then roughly chop the flesh. Cut the bread into big chunks. Put everything into a bowl, rub the mugwort leaves with your fingers over the top if using. Coarsely crush the peppercorns with a pestle and mortar. Season the stuffing with salt, pepper, bay leaves and caraway seeds.

4 Season the goose inside and out with salt. Put the stuffing into the cavity, close the opening with wooden toothpicks or needle and twine. Put the goose breast down into a deep baking tray, place the belly fat on top, pour over 1 litre of hot water. Cook the goose in the oven (centre) for 2 hours 30 minutes, frequently basting with some of the juices. Turn the goose, cook for another 2 hours.

5 In the meantime, prepare the sauce. Peel the onions, carrot and celeriac and cut into 1 cm cubes. Heat the oil in a wide saucepan. Add the vegetables and the onions and fry for 3 minutes. Add the bones, stir in the tomato purée, fry for another 3 minutes. Pour in a dash of red wine, cook to reduce, then dust everything with the flour. Repeat this process twice. Pour in the remaining wine, the goose stock or meat stock, and the juices from roasting the bones, bring to the boil and simmer the sauce gently for 2 hours over low heat. After about 1 hour, add the bay leaves, peppercorns, juniper berries, allspice berries and the mugwort if using.

6 Take the goose out of the oven, turn the oven to its grill function (top level). Drain the cooking juices through a sieve into a saucepan. To carve the goose, cut the legs and the breast flesh away from the carcass, and place the pieces skin side up back onto the tray. Combine 1 teaspoon of salt and 4 tablespoons of hot water, then use to brush the meat pieces with the salt water. Put into the oven (centre) and grill for 10–15 minutes until golden brown and crisp, brushing several times with the salt water while grilling.

7 Meanwhile strain the sauce through a fine sieve, catching the liquid, then return it to the saucepan. Add the orange zest and bring the sauce to the boil. Depending on consistency, cook over high heat for 5–10 minutes until velvety. Remove the orange zest, check the seasoning, adding salt if necessary.

8 Take the crisp goose breasts and legs out of the oven, cut into portion-sized pieces and arrange on warm plates or on a pretty platter with the sauce and serve. Excellent accompaniments for this dish are potato dumplings (p.88) and red cabbage (p.200) or celeriac salad (p.207). Connoisseurs heat through the roasting juices and drizzle them over their dumplings and the meat.

USEFUL TIP

If your goose is heavier than the one in this recipe, simply adjust the cooking time. For a goose of 5 kg plus, calculate about 1 hour of cooking time per kilogram of goose. To check whether your goose is cooked, stick a wooden toothpick into the meat between breast and leg. If the juice that escapes is clear, the goose is done. If not, leave it to cook in the oven a little longer.

J&B

FARMYARD DUCK

The grilled ducks at the Munich Oktoberfest are a real insider's tip. They should be served with the proper sauce, of course, and this can be prepared a few days ahead of time.

AROMATIC AND CRISPY

SERVES 4:

For the duck and stuffing:

2 young farm ducks (c. 2 kg each)
1 onion
1 tart apple (e.g. Braeburn)
1 organic orange
4 sprigs marjoram
4 sprigs parsley
salt | freshly ground black pepper
a few wooden toothpicks or kitchen twine and needle

For the sauce:

500 g duck bones (pre-order from your butcher and have them chopped small)
2 onions
1 carrot
1 piece celeriac (c. 150 g)
200 ml full-bodied red wine (e.g. Cabernet Sauvignon)
100 ml red port
2 tbsp vegetable oil
2 tbsp tomato purée
1.2 l duck stock or meat stock (from a jar)
3 sprigs thyme
1 tbsp cornflour
2 sprigs marjoram
1 tbsp orange marmalade
salt | freshly ground black pepper

HOW LONG IT TAKES: c. 1 hour
IN THE OVEN: c. 3 hours 10 min
PER SERVING:
c. 2015 kcal | 148 g p | 143 g f | 19 g ch

1 Preheat the oven to 200°C (convection is best, or use 220°C top and bottom heat). If necessary, remove the offal from the duck cavities. Pat the ducks dry with kitchen paper. (The offal can be used as described in the tips.) Cut off and roughly chop the wing bones and the necks. Cut off and discard the parson's noses.

2 To make the sauce, place the duck bones and the wings and necks on a baking tray, put in the oven (centre) and roast for about 30 minutes until golden, turning the bones occasionally. Take the tray out of the oven and set aside the bones. Reduce the oven temperature to 120°C (convection, 140°C top and bottom heat).

3 Meanwhile, make the stuffing. Peel and roughly dice the onion. Wash and quarter the apples, remove the cores and roughly chop the flesh. Wash the orange under hot water and roughly dice it. Rinse and shake dry the herbs, then chop together with the stems. Put everything into a bowl and combine. Season with salt and pepper.

4 Season the ducks inside with salt and pepper, only use salt on the outsides. Divide the stuffing between the cavities, close the openings with wooden toothpicks or needle and twine. Place the ducks breast-side down on a deep baking tray and pour in ¾ litres of hot water. Put the ducks into the oven (centre) and roast for about 1 hour 10 minutes. During this time, repeatedly spoon over some of the roasting juices. Turn the ducks over, breast-side up, and roast for another 1 hour 50 minutes.

5 Meanwhile, prepare the sauce. Peel the onions, carrot and celeriac and cut into 1 cm cubes. Combine the red wine and the port. Heat the oil in a wide saucepan, add the vegetables and the onions and fry for 3 minutes. Add the bones, stir in the tomato purée and cook for another 3 minutes. Pour in a dash of wine and cook to reduce. Repeat this process twice. Now pour in the remaining wine and the stock. Rinse the thyme and add. Bring the sauce to the boil, then simmer gently for 2 hours over low heat.

6 Take the ducks out of the oven and turn the oven to the grill function (highest level). Drain the roasting juices from the baking tray. Halve the ducks lengthways, remove the stuffings and cut away the backbones. Place the duck halves with their skin sides up onto the baking tray. Combine 1 teaspoon of salt and 4 tablespoons of hot water, then brush the duck skin with the salt water. Put the tray into the oven (centre) and grill, brushing them occasionally wth the salt water, for about 10 minutes until golden and crispy.

7 Meanwhile, drain the sauce through a fine sieve, catching the liquid and returning it to the saucepan. Cook the sauce over high heat for about 5 minutes to reduce. Stir the cornflour into 2–3 tablespoons of cold water. Gradually add the cornflour water to the sauce until it is velvety, then cook for another 3 minutes. Rinse and shake dry the marjoram, pull off and finely chop the leaves and stir into the sauce with the marmalade. Season with salt and pepper.

8 Take the crispy duck halves out of the oven, arrange on the plates with the sauce and serve. This tastes delicious with potato dumplings (p.88) and red cabbage (p.200).

USEFUL TIPS

If you like, you can cook the offal. You can serve the livers as a starter, for example. Simply season them with salt and pepper, turn them in a little flour and fry briefly on both sides in a little butter. Serve on small plates with a dressed lamb's lettuce as a garnish. The hearts and the stomachs can be added to the sauce and simmered after you have poured in the wine and the stock.

To test whether the ducks are cooked, insert a wooden skewer into the flesh between the breast and the leg. The meat should be tender and any juices that escape should be clear.

"THE WEEK IS OFF TO A GREAT START, ON MONDAY I GET MY HEAD CHOPPED OFF." (Mathias Kneissl)

OFF HUNTING

It is said that Bavarians are not a particularly rebellious, let alone revolutionary people. If they're left alone, they generally leave others alone too, even if they do go about it in their habitually dour, surly manner. They only get truly riled if someone pushes them over the edge. It happens occasionally, particularly when, after intense beer consumption, talk turns to their homeland and nature, to property and territory – but that's another story.

The legendary hunters and poachers in Bavaria's forests, on the other hand, have always had a rebellious side – even though they never had to show it on a large scale, but rather only in small revolts against the authority and personal freedom afforded to the nobility.

Bavaria has by far the most woodland of any German state. More than one third of it is covered in trees. Some 100 years or so ago, you literally couldn't see Bavaria's forest for its trees. And it provided virtually everything needed for human survival: wood for building houses and furniture and for keeping warm inside, meat from the many animals of the forest including deer, wild boars, hares and pheasants – but of course it also harboured the odd robber.

Bavarian literary figures like Ludwig Ganghofer and Ludwig Thoma made good use of the tales surrounding legendary poachers such as the robbers Mathias Kneissl and Georg Jennerwein, considered to be Schliersee's Robin Hood and "a proud marksman in his prime". Their heroes expertly slew game like true huntsmen before selling the meat to innkeepers or gifting it to farming families in need. In doing so, they broke a law which stipulated that game could only be hunted by landowners and that it must always be protected from the common folk. There needed to be enough game available at all times for the needs of the exclusive hunting parties.

Before being prosecuted by the authorities for ignoring this law, the wild lads would be fiercely protected by the commoners, whose alarm system consisted of a special signal: a yodelled alert. If the yodeller began to sing in reach of a poacher, guns would be quickly dismantled, barrels removed, and even shoe soles would be reversed. All this just to mess with and mislead the royal hunters and police. But despite the dramatic alpine backdrop, with its rushing streams and densely wooded, craggy peaks, life for the fearless outdoor venturers was nothing like the wildly romantic tales of folklore, particularly given its often inevitably unpleasant end. Poaching was considered a crime against the king, and was therefore punishable by cutting off one or both hands, many years of compulsory labour, or even death by hanging.

Today, fortunately, venison consumption has become a democratic pleasure, one that can be indulged in and celebrated at any of the Bavarian eateries during the hunting season in spring and autumn. For the game and wild stories from Bavaria's forests are matched in richness by the exquisite venison recipes found in its cuisine.

ROAST VENISON

After a long closed period, May heralds the start of the hunting season for roebucks. And at last gourmets can enjoy game again.

FESTIVE FOOD WITH LOTS OF MEAT STOCK

SERVES 4:

1 onion
1 carrot
1 piece celeriac (c. 150 g)
4 sprigs thyme
1.2 kg boned leg of venison
salt | freshly ground black pepper
1 tsp ground game spice mix
2 good pinches of flour
3 tbsp vegetable oil
2 tbsp tomato purée
½ l full-bodied red wine
(e.g. Cabernet Sauvignon)
1 l venison stock (from a jar)
1 tsp juniper berries
1 tsp black peppercorns
1 tsp cornflour
2 tbsp redcurrant jelly
2 tbsp double cream
Plus: kitchen twine

HOW LONG IT TAKES: c. 30 min
IN THE SAUCEPAN: c. 2 hours 20 min
PER SERVING: c. 640 kcal | 78 g p | 18 g f | 15 g ch

1 Peel the onion, carrot and celeriac and cut into 1 cm cubes. Rinse and shake dry the thyme. Wash the venison leg and thoroughly pat dry with kitchen paper. If necessary, remove any sinews and tendons from the meat, shape the joint and tie it with kitchen twine. Season the meat generously with salt, pepper and the game spice mixture, then dust with flour.

2 Heat the oil in a casserole. Add the meat and fry for 2 minutes, turn and fry for another 4 minutes to brown all over. Take out of the casserole.

3 Put the onion, vegetables and tomato purée into the casserole, and fry for 3–4 minutes in the meat juices. Add a dash of red wine and cook to reduce for 3 minutes. Repeat this process twice. Return the meat to the casserole, pour in the remaining wine and the venison stock, bring to the boil and cook for 3 minutes. Add the thyme, juniper berries and peppercorns, cover and cook over a low heat for about 2 hours until tender.

4 Take the meat out of the casserole. Strain the sauce through a fine sieve, catching the liquid and returning it to the casserole, bring to the boil. Combine the cornflour with 2–3 tablespoons of cold water, then stir into the sauce. Cook over medium heat for about 20 minutes until velvety. Stir the redcurrant jelly and the cream into the sauce. Return the meat to the sauce and bring to the boil, then take off the stove and leave to cook in the residual heat.

5 Remove the twine from the venison leg and cut the meat into 1 cm slices. Arrange on warm plates with the sauce and serve. Good accompaniments for this dish are serviette dumplings (p.90) or bread dumplings (p.89) and creamy Savoy cabbage (p.203). If you like, you could also put a jar of cranberry sauce on the table. Also good: Garnish the venison leg with fried chanterelle mushrooms (p.114).

BRAISED SHOULDER OF VENISON

For tender cuts, cooking on the bone is a good option. It makes the natural flavour of the meat and the braising sauce more intense – and the venison shoulders will remain nice and juicy.

RUSTIC BUT SOPHISTICATED

SERVES 4:

1 large onion
1 large carrot
1 parsley root
1 piece celeriac (c. 250 g)
4 shoulders of venison (c. 700 g each)
salt | freshly ground black pepper
1 tbsp flour | 4 tbsp vegetable oil
2 tbsp tomato purée
½ l full-bodied red wine (e.g. Cabernet Sauvignon)
1.2 l venison stock (from a jar)
3 cloves | a pinch of caraway seeds
1 tsp allspice berries
½ tsp yellow mustard seeds
½ tsp coriander seeds
1 tsp juniper berries
1 tsp black peppercorns
a pinch of dried thyme
2 bay leaves
3 tsp cornflour
2–3 tbsp elderberry or cranberry jelly
Plus: kitchen twine

HOW LONG IT TAKES: c. 40 min
IN THE SAUCEPAN: c. 2 hours 10 min
PER SERVING: c. 1050 kcal | 133 g p | 35 g f | 22 g ch

1 Peel the onion, carrot, parsley root and celeriac and cut into 1 cm cubes. Cut through the venison shoulders at the joint and divide each one into two pieces. Tie the meat joints into shape with kitchen twine, then season generously all over with salt and pepper and dust with the flour.

2 In a casserole heat 3 tablespoons of oil. Add half the meat pieces and fry for 2 minutes, turn and fry for another 1 minute. Remove the pieces from the casserole. Add the remaining oil, fry the remaining meat pieces in the same way, then take them out.

3 Put the onion and the vegetables into the casserole and fry for 3 minutes. Stir in the tomato purée and cook for 3 minutes. Add a good dash of red wine and cook to reduce. Repeat this process twice. Pour in the remaining wine and the venison stock, place the meat into the casserole and bring to the boil. With a pestle and mortar, coarsely crush the cloves, caraway seeds, allspice berries, mustard seeds, coriander seeds, juniper berries and peppercorns. Stir into the sauce together with the thyme and the bay leaves. Cover and braise the venison shoulders for about 1 hour 50 minutes until tender, turning the pieces from time to time in the sauce.

4 Take the meat out of the casserole. Strain the sauce through a fine sieve, catching it and return it to the casserole. Skim off any fat with a ladle if necessary. Cook the sauce over medium heat for about 20 minutes. Stir the cornflour into 2–3 tablespoons of cold water. Gradually add only as much cornflour as needed to make the sauce velvety, then cook for another 3 minutes. Flavour with elderberry or cranberry jelly, return the meat to the sauce and cook for another 3 minutes. Check the seasoning.

5 In farmhouse style, arrange the venison shoulders on the bone on warm plates with the sauce and serve. Excellent with serviette dumplings (p.90).

VENISON STEAKS WITH CRANBERRIES

The fruity sweetness and the unique taste of cranberries make for an excellent marriage with game dishes. To ensure that both of these qualities as well as the intense red colour remain unadulterated the berries are combined with preserving sugar in a food processor and not cooked in the casserole.

SOMETHING SPECIAL

SERVES 4:

For the berries (c. 450 g):

300 g cranberries
150 g jam sugar (2 : 1)

For the steaks:

2 saddles of venison (c. 350 g each)
salt | freshly ground black pepper
5 pinches ground wild game seasoning
1 tbsp vegetable oil
5 juniper berries | 3 sprigs thyme
1 tsp tomato purée
5 allspice berries | 1 bay leaf
100 ml full-bodied red wine (e.g. Cabernet Sauvignon)
400 ml venison stock (from a jar)
½ tsp black peppercorns
1 tsp cornflour
100 g cream | 1 tbsp butter

HOW LONG IT TAKES: c. 1 hour 20 min
PER SERVING: c. 590 kcal | 42 g p | 20 g f | 52 g ch

1 Pick over the cranberries, put them into a sieve, wash and leave to drain. Put the berries into the bowl of a food processor together with the preserving sugar, then process on a low setting for about 1 hour.

2 Meanwhile, preheat the oven to 150°C (use top and bottom heat, convection is not recommended). If necessary, remove any sinews from the steaks, season with salt, pepper and game seasoning. Heat the oil in a large frying pan. Add the meat and fry over medium heat for 1 minute, turn and fry all over for another 1 minute. Place both fillets onto a rack and put into the oven (centre), placing a baking tray as a drip guard underneath. Cook the fillets for about 35 minutes until "pink", turning them frequently.

3 Crush the juniper berries with a pestle and mortar, rinse and shake dry the thyme. Put the tomato purée into the pan and fry for 1 minute, then stir in the juniper berries, allspice berries and the bay leaf. Pour in the wine, add 1 thyme sprig, cook for 2 minutes to reduce. Pour in the venison stock and bring to the boil, then cook the sauce over low heat for about 8 minutes to reduce. Coarsely crush the peppercorns with the pestle and mortar.

4 Stir the cornflour into 2–3 tablespoons of cold water, stir it into the sauce and cook for 1 minute. Add the cream, bring to the boil and cook for about 3 minutes until velvety. Strain the sauce through a fine sieve into a saucepan, pressing through the contents of the sieve. Season the sauce with salt, crushed peppercorns and 2 teaspoons of cranberries.

5 Take the fillets out of the oven, leave to rest for 5 minutes. Melt butter in the pan, add the remaining thyme. Place the meat into the thyme butter and fry over medium heat for 1 minute. Carve the meat and serve with the sauce and with the cranberries (put the remainder into a clean jar, seal and chill for later use). Tastes particularly good with serviette dumplings (p.90), finger gnocchi (p.93) or a creamy potato gratin (p.94).

WILD BOAR GOULASH

A wonderful dish for the cold days of autumn and winter. The meat has a particular affinity for spices like cinnamon, allspice, cloves and black pepper – which are a favourite flavour at this time of year. So don't just add them to your mulled wine!

WILD BOAR WITH FINESSE

SERVES 4:

1 large onion
1 garlic clove
1 small carrot
1 piece celeriac (c. 80 g)
1 parsley root
3 sprigs thyme
1.2 kg wild boar shoulder
salt | freshly ground black pepper
1 tsp ground game seasoning
3 good pinches of flour
3 tbsp vegetable oil
300 ml ruby port
450 ml full-bodied red wine (e.g. Cabernet Sauvignon)
2 tbsp tomato purée
1.5 l venison stock (from a jar, or ready-made beef stock)
2 bay leaves
1 level tsp gingerbread spice mix

HOW LONG IT TAKES: c. 40 min
IN THE SAUCEPAN: c. 2 hours 50 min
PER SERVING: c. 850 kcal | 64 g p | 36 g f | 19 g ch

1 Peel and finely dice the onion, the garlic and the vegetables. Rinse and shake dry the thyme. Cut the wild boar shoulder into 2 cm cubes. Season the meat cubes with salt, pepper and game seasoning, then dust evenly with flour.

2 Heat the oil in a casserole. Add the meat cubes and fry for 3 minutes, turn and fry for another 3 minutes. Boil off any liquid that escapes from them – this may take as long as 10 minutes. Combine the port and the red wine.

3 Add the onion, garlic and vegetable cubes and fry everything for another 2 minutes. Stir in the tomato purée and fry for 4 minutes, stirring constantly. Add a dash of wine and cook to reduce. Repeat this process twice. Pour in the stock and the remaining wine, bring to the boil and simmer the goulash over low heat for about 2 hours.

4 Add the thyme, bay leaves and gingerbread spice to the goulash, cook for another 50 minutes until the meat is tender. The cooking time may vary depending on the quality of the meat. Start to check early on whether the meat is tender and well cooked by pushing a fork into the meat.

5 Lift the meat pieces out of the casserole when the goulash is done. Strain the sauce through a fine sieve, catching the liquid and returning it to the pan. Depending on the desired consistency, cook for 5–10 minutes until reduced and velvety. Return the meat to the sauce, bring to the boil again, then check and adjust the seasoning with salt and pepper. The wild boar goulash is particularly delicious with a side dish of serviette dumplings (p.90) or pretzel dumplings (p.91) and creamy Savoy cabbage (p.203).

RACK OF LAMB WITH RUNNER BEANS

Tender lamb tastes best if cooked on the bone. The bones protect the flesh from drying out and also provide a lot of flavour. And of course a whole rack does always look a bit special.

IT DOESN'T JUST LOOK GOOD

SERVES 4:

For the racks:

4 racks of lamb (c. 350g each, French-trimmed and without the fat)
salt | freshly ground black pepper
2 tbsp vegetable oil
80 g toast (without crusts)
4 sprigs flat-leaved parsley
4 tbsp soft butter
4 tsp medium-hot mustard
2 pinches dried savory

For the beans:

500 g runner beans
salt
1 small onion
2 tbsp butter
½ tsp black peppercorns

HOW LONG IT TAKES: c. 50 min
PER SERVING: c. 595 kcal | 37 g p | 42 g f | 16 g ch

1 Preheat the oven to 80°C (use top and bottom heat, convection is not recommended). Season the lamb racks with salt and pepper. Heat the oil in a large frying pan. Add the meat and fry over high heat for 2 minutes, turn and fry for another 2–3 minutes to brown all over. Place the racks onto a rack and put them into the oven (centre), putting a baking tray underneath as drip guard. Roast the lamb racks for about 30 minutes until "pink".

2 Meanwhile, tear the toast into chunks, put these into a tall mixing container and process to find breadcrumbs with a handheld mixer. Rinse and shake dry the parsley, pull off the leaves, add them to the breadcrumbs and purée together. Beat the softened butter with the whisks of the mixer for 3 minutes until light and creamy, stir in the mustard and combine with the breadcrumb and parsley mix. Season with the savory, salt and pepper, set aside.

3 Wash and trim the runner beans and cut them diagonally into 3 cm lengths. Cook the beans in boiling salted water for about 8 minutes until soft. Drain into a sieve, rinse under ice-cold water and leave to drain. Peel and finely dice the onion. Melt the butter in a frying pan. Add the onion and fry for about 5 minutes until light brown. Add the beans and warm through for about 3 minutes, stirring constantly. Coarsely crush the peppercorns in a mortar, season the beans with salt and pepper.

4 Take the lamb out of the oven. Turn the oven to the grill function (highest level). Coat the top of the lamb racks with the crumb butter, put the tray back into the oven (top) and grill the racks for 3–5 minutes until golden brown. Take out of the oven and leave the racks to rest for a short while, then slice them between the bones. Arrange on the plates with the beans and serve – best with creamy potato gratin (p.94) or fried potatoes. Also good with horseradish, freshly grated over the lamb and beans.

RED CABBAGE

Aside from dumplings and such like, vegetable side dishes are just as important as meat or fish to the Bavarians, and they are particularly keen on cabbage.

FRUITY AND FLAVOURSOME

SERVES 4:

1 red cabbage (c. 1 kg)
salt | 2 tbsp sugar
10 juniper berries
4 cloves
3 bay leaves
2 pinches ground caraway seeds
½ l dry red wine
2 tbsp cider vinegar
freshly squeezed juice of ½ orange
2 onions
4 tbsp vegetable oil
1 tart apple (e.g. Boskoop)
1 piece marzipan (c. 30 g)
200 g apple sauce (with chunks)
freshly ground black pepper

HOW LONG IT TAKES: c. 20 min
IN THE SAUCEPAN: c. 1 hour 30 min
PER SERVING:
c. 350 kcal | 4 g p | 13 g f | 37 g ch

1 Trim the red cabbage. Halve the head lengthways and cut out the central stem. Cut or shave the cabbage halves into thin strips. Season with 1 tablespoon of salt, sugar, juniper berries, cloves, bay leaves and caraway seeds. Add the red wine, cider vinegar and orange juice to the cabbage and knead through.

2 Peel and halve the onions, then cut them into thin strips. Heat the oil in a large, wide saucepan. Add the onions and fry for about 3 minutes until translucent. Add the red cabbage together with any liquid, stir, cover and simmer over medium heat for about 30 minutes.

3 Peel and quarter the apple, remove the core and thinly slice the flesh. Break the marzipan into small pieces. Combine the apple, marzipan and the apple purée with the red cabbage and cook for 1 hour until tender. Check and adjust the seasoning with salt and pepper, serve. Red cabbage goes particularly well with a beef pot roast (p.170), games dishes, a St Martin's goose (p.180) and farmyard ducks (p.184).

USEFUL TIP

While cutting or working with red cabbage it's best to wear disposable gloves – the cabbage stains your hands!

BAVARIAN CABBAGE

This Bavarian sweet cabbage is an absolute classic, delicious with roast pork or pork knuckle.

AROMATIC AND SLIGHTLY SWEET

SERVES 4:

1 head pointed cabbage or young white cabbage (c. 1.2 kg)
1 onion
1 tbsp brown sugar
salt
100 ml dry white wine
300 ml vegetable stock
½ bunch flat-leaved parsley
2 tsp cornflour
freshly ground black pepper
2 pinches of ground caraway or caraway seeds
1 tsp white wine vinegar

HOW LONG IT TAKES: c. 20 min
IN THE SAUCEPAN: c. 20 min
PER SERVING:
c. 105 kcal | 5 g p | 1 g f | 14 g ch

1 Trim the cabbage, halve the head lengthways and cut out the central stem. Cut the cabbage leaves into about 2 cm diamonds. Peel and finely dice the onion.

2 Melt the sugar in a large, wide saucepan over medium heat and caramelize for about 3 minutes until light brown. Add the onion and fry briefly. Add the cabbage, fry for about 1 minute, stirring constantly, season with salt. Pour in the wine and cook for 1 minute to reduce. Pour in the stock, bring to the boil, cover and simmer the cabbage for about 20 minutes over low heat until soft.

3 Rinse and shake dry the parsley, pull off and roughly chop the leaves. Stir the cornflour into 2–3 tablespoons of cold water, add to the cabbage and simmer for about 3 minutes until velvety. Season with salt, pepper, caraway and wine vinegar. Sprinkle with the chopped parsley and serve.

USEFUL TIP

The Bavarian cabbage tastes even better when reheated. So why not prepare ahead, the evening before the meal? Just leave out the parsley – it's best added at the end.

SAUERKRAUT

In the olden days, sauerkraut was made by finely grating the cabbage by hand and layering it in a large cabbage barrel with salt, spices and water. It was stamped down by foot or with a tamper and then weighed down. Today we have more modern methods, but the cabbage still gets its typical flavour and long shelf-life through lactic fermentation.

HEARTY AND RUSTIC

SERVES 4:

1 kg fresh sauerkraut
1 large onion
1 tbsp clarified butter or lard
100 g smoked pork belly (streaky bacon)
200 ml dry white wine
½ l vegetable stock
salt
1 tbsp sugar
2 bay leaves
10 juniper berries

HOW LONG IT TAKES: c. 20 min
IN THE SAUCEPAN: c. 3 hours
PER SERVING:
c. 190 kcal | 9 g p | 8 g f | 9 g ch

1 Put the sauerkraut into a sieve, loosen it with your fingers or a fork, briefly rinse under cold water, leave to drain. Peel and halve the onion, then cut it into thin strips.

2 In a large, wide saucepan, heat the clarified butter or lard. Add the onion and fry over medium heat for about 8 minutes. Add the sauerkraut and the pork belly (the whole piece) to the saucepan and fry for 1 minute. Pour in the white wine and the vegetable stock and bring to the boil.

3 Season the sauerkraut with salt and sugar, stir in the bay leaves and the juniper berries. Cover and simmer the sauerkraut over low heat for about 3 hours until soft, stirring occasionally. Check the finished dish for seasoning with salt, then serve. Tastes delicious with fresh black pudding and liverwurst (see tip, p.63), finger gnocchi (p.93) or, with a little cream stirred in, with fried pike-perch.

USEFUL TIP

Sauerkraut tastes even better when reheated so it's a good idea to prepare it a day or two ahead of eating.

CREAMY SAVOY CABBAGE

Savoy cabbage can be prepared in all sorts of ways – whether in a soup, as a side dish, in a gratin or as stuffed leaves. It should always be cooked until nice and soft for this brings out its full flavour and it also makes the vegetable easier to digest.

CREAMY AND AROMATIC
SERVES 4:
½ Savoy cabbage (c. 600 g)
salt
1 small onion
2 tbsp butter
200 g cream
freshly ground black pepper
freshly grated nutmeg

HOW LONG IT TAKES: c. 30 min
PER SERVING:
c. 225 kcal | 5 g p | 21 g f | 5 g ch

1 Trim the Savoy cabbage, halve the cabbage lengthways and cut out the central stem. Separate and wash the leaves, shake them dry and cut into thin strips. Blanch the cabbage in plenty of salted water for about 6 minutes, then drain and rinse under ice-cold water and drain again. Meanwhile, peel and then finely dice the onion.

2 Melt the butter in a wide saucepan. Add the onion and fry for 3 minutes until translucent. Add the cabbage strips, fry for 2 minutes. Pour in the cream and cook for 3 minutes to reduce until velvety. Season with salt, pepper and nutmeg, serve. This Savoy cabbage tastes great with boiled beef or game dishes.

OR TRY THIS: SAVOY PURÉE

Remove the stem from 800 g Savoy cabbage, roughly chop the leaves and cook in salted water for about 14 minutes until soft. Drain and rinse under cold water, drain again and squeeze out. Finely purée the cabbage, a little at a time, with an electric blender. Peel and finely dice 1 onion, sauté in 1 tablespoon of butter for 3 minutes. Pour in 200 g cream, cook for 2 minutes to reduce. Stir in the cabbage and simmer over low heat for 5 minutes. Fold 1 tablespoon of butter in small pats into the purée. Season with salt, pepper and nutmeg.

Beans may seem everyday and salsify wildly exotic. But if cooked in the right way and well seasoned both can become the finishing touch to many a main course.

BEANS WITH BREADCRUMBS

SPECIALLY PREPARED

SERVES 4:

500 g French beans
salt | 1 small onion
1 dry slice toast
4 sprigs flat-leaved parsley
4 tbsp butter
freshly ground black pepper
freshly grated nutmeg

HOW LONG IT TAKES: c. 30 min
PER SERVING: c. 130 kcal | 3 g p | 9 g f | 9 g ch

1 Wash the beans and snip off the ends. Put the beans into plenty of boiling salted water and cook for about 8 minutes until soft, then drain in a sieve and leave to drip dry (see tips, p.130).

2 Peel and finely dice the onion. Roughly pull the toast apart, put it into a tall container and chop finely with a handheld blender. Rinse and shake dry the parsley, pull off and roughly chop the leaves.

3 In a large frying pan, melt 2 tablespoons of butter. Add the onion and sauté for about 2 minutes until translucent. Add the remaining butter and sprinkle in the breadcrumbs, then sauté for 1 minute. Add the beans and sauté for another 3 minutes, stirring everything frequently.

4 Stir the parsley into the beans and season with salt, pepper and nutmeg. These beans go well with a fried rack of lamb, fillet of beef or with a pork chop.

CREAMY SALSIFY

WINTERY AND GOOD

SERVES 4:

4 thick salsify roots (c. 800 g)
freshly squeezed juice of 1 lemon
1 sachet dumpling aid (5 g) | 2 tbsp butter
1 tsp sugar | salt | 100 ml vegetable stock
100 g cream | 4 sprigs flat-leaved parsley
freshly ground black pepper
freshly grated nutmeg

HOW LONG IT TAKES: c. 30 min
PER SERVING: c. 150 kcal | 3 g p | 13 g f | 5 g ch

1 Wash the salsify, scrubbing them with a vegetable brush, then peel the roots (best to wear disposable gloves for this so that the milky sap that escapes doesn't touch your skin). Put the roots immediately into a bowl with water, the lemon juice and the dumpling aid. Cut the roots into ½ cm slices.

2 Melt the butter in a saucepan. Add the sugar, melt and caramelize for 1 minute until light brown. Stir in the salsify, season lightly with salt and sauté over low heat for 4 minutes. Pour in the stock and bring to the boil. Cover and cook the salsify slices for 10–12 minutes until soft. Pour in the cream and cook for 3 minutes to reduce until velvety.

3 Rinse and shake dry the parsley, roughly chop and stir into the salsify. Season with salt, pepper and nutmeg. Salsify make a delicious side dish for saddle of vension or other game dishes.

These aromatic roots pack quite a punch. Celeriac is the base of many soups and sauces, while beetroot boasts a stunningly unique colour. If you are boiling beetroot, make sure you do not cut the skin – otherwise they will "bleed" dark red juices and dry out. Both vegetables are beneficial as they help you digest substantial meals.

COOKED CELERIAC SALAD

SIMPLE AND GOOD

SERVES 4:
½ celeriac (c. 850 g)
salt
1 tsp vegetable stock granules
1 small onion
4 tbsp white vinegar
freshly ground black pepper
2 pinches of sugar
4 tbsp vegetable oil

HOW LONG IT TAKES: c. 15 min
IN THE SAUCEPAN: c. 30 min
MARINATING: c. 1 hour
PER SERVING: c. 130 kcal | 3 g p | 10 g f | 5 g ch

1 Peel and quarter the celeriac. Fill a saucepan with water, bring to the boil, season generously with salt and the stock granules. Put the celeriac into the stock, bring to the boil again, cover and simmer over low heat for about 30 minutes until soft.

2 Lift the celeriac out of the cooking liquid, measure off 200 ml of the stock. Divide the celeriac pieces lengthways if very large, then cut into ½ cm slices crossways. Transfer to a bowl. Peel and finely dice the onion, then sprinkle over the celeriac.

3 Flavour the stock with the vinegar, salt, pepper and sugar, stirring in the oil at the end. Pour the dressing over the hot celeriac slices, leave the salad to marinate for about 1 hour, check the seasoning. This salad goes particularly well with roast goose (p.180) or farmhouse duck (p.184).

COOKED BEETROOT SALAD

COLOURFUL AND GOOD FOR YOU

SERVES 4:
6 beetroot (c. 850 g) | salt
2 tsp caraway seeds | 1 onion
150 ml vegetable stock | 6 tbsp cider vinegar
1 tsp sugar | freshly ground black pepper
4 tbsp vegetable oil | a pinch of freshly grated horseradish

HOW LONG IT TAKES: c. 20 min
IN THE SAUCEPAN: c. 1 hour 30 min
MARINATING: c. 20 min
PER SERVING: c. 170 kcal | 3 g p | 10 g f | 16 g ch

1 Wash the beetroot, put them into a tall saucepan, cover with plenty of water, then season with salt and 1 teaspoon of caraway seeds. Cover, bring to the boil and cook for 1 hour 30 minutes until soft. Do not stab the skin – otherwise the beets will "bleed" out.

2 Peel and finely dice the onion. Heat the stock to lukewarm and flavour it with the vinegar, sugar, salt, pepper and remaining caraway seeds. Stir in the oil.

3 Take the beetroot out of the water, leave to cool, then peel (wear disposable gloves as beetroot will stain your hands). Halve the beets, cut them into ½ cm slices and transfer to a bowl. Sprinkle with the onion and the horseradish, pour over the dressing. Combine well and leave to marinate for 20 minutes, check the seasoning. Goes well with roast goose (p.180), duck (p.184) and pork roast (p.71).

THE SILENT TIME OF YEAR

Rowdy and relaxed, noisy and silent – both are part of Bavarian culture. Throughout the year, the region celebrates with strident brass music; it banishes evil spirits with deafening noise during its Perchten New Year's processions and thundering gun salutes. This is in stark contrast to the tranquillity of Advent, which heralds the year's end. In former times, the winter would be a time of rest in the farming year: the crops had been harvested and the fields prepared; time for a break and reflection.

This silent period starts with St Martin's Day on 11 November and ends on 6 January with the Three Kings, Epiphany. It is a time in which Bavaria observes numerous pre-Christian traditions, from Twelfth Night, to traditional visits to neighbours, and family "Stubenmusi" (folk music played at home) with harps and zithers, to Christmas itself, when the Christ child visits the family. And what could be cosier on a wintry December day than a warm living room – out of the storms, snow, frosts, bone-chilling damp mist and icy easterly wind.

Advent rituals vary depending on the region. The parades and processions of singing and praying during the Klöpfelesnächte (carol-singing nights) on Andreasabend (St Andrew's Day), for instance, date back to pre-Christian times. And this custom of knocking at other people's doors had a prophetic element: if you knocked on the stable walls at the right time, you would hear the animals predict who would die the coming year. The tradition later changed to begging for gifts. At twilight on the last three Thursdays before Christmas Eve, children in Upper Bavaria would go from house to house, knocking on doors, singing Christmas carols, and expressing their good wishes in exchange for Christmas cookies, apples and nuts.

The night of 5 December is a special event during this contemplative time, for it is when St Nicholas and his beastly side-kick Krampus visit the houses. Good children receive sweets from St Nicholas, while the naughty ones are punished by Krampus.

Many of the old rites and customs surrounding the nights on and after the winter solstice in the alpine lands revolve around a belief in spirits and demons, who were thought to be holding the sun captive, as well as people's efforts to release it again. On the last of these Holy Nights, on 5 January, the night before Epiphany, the people in the Berchtesgaden region (as well as in Tyrol and Vorarlberg) parade through the streets in their scary costumes and creepy Perchten masks, creating an almighty din with their bells. And they make good use of their sticks too. The "Kramperltratzn" is a test of courage for children, who pull on the figures' robes or rile them. But they need to make sure they aren't caught and beaten with sticks. Thus, magic powers can usher in the year's end as well as new beginnings.

CHRISTMAS FRUIT BREAD

In Bavaria this bread is known as Kletzenbrot – Kletzen are the dark brown, whole, dried pears that are among its many ingredients. There are plenty of other dried fruits in this deliciously moist bread. They should all be of top quality because that's the only way the delicious flavour can fully develop.

AN OLD CHRISTMAS FAVOURITE

MAKES 5 LOAVES (c. 650 g each):
500 g flour
2 pinches of brown sugar
2 pinches of salt
75 g natural sourdough starter (buy ready-made online)
10 g fresh yeast
400 g soft dried pears
250 g currants | 250 g sultanas
2 tbsp rum
400 g prunes (without stones)
250 g dried figs
100 g each of candied lemon and orange zest
150 g hazelnuts
1 organic orange | 1 organic lemon
3 pinches of ground aniseeds
2 pinches of ground cloves
3 pinches of ground allspice berries
2 pinches of freshly ground black pepper
flour for working
Plus:
baking paper
2 baking trays

HOW LONG IT TAKES: c. 1 hour 15 min
RESTING: c. 13 hours
IN THE OVEN: c. 1 hour
PER BREAD: c. 1475 kcal | 25 g p | 23 g f | 281 g ch

1 Put the flour with the sugar and the salt into the bowl of a food processor, then add the sourdough. Crumble the yeast into 300 ml lukewarm water, stir with a whisk to combine and pour onto the flour. Using the kneading hooks of a handheld mixer, beat the mixture for about 5 minutes until you have a smooth dough. Dust the dough with a little flour, cover with clingfilm and leave to rise in the fridge for about 12 hours (or better leave it overnight).

2 Put the dried pears into a bowl, cover with lukewarm water, cover the bowl. Put the currants and sultanas into a second bowl, combine with the rum, cover. Leave both to soak and swell for 12 hours.

3 The next day, finely dice the prunes and the figs. Chop the candied lemon and orange as finely as possible. Roughly slice the hazelnuts, put them into a hot frying pan and dry-roast for about 4 minutes over medium heat. Put into a colander and shake to scrape off all remaining skins. Take the nuts out.

4 Wash the orange and the lemon under hot water and pat dry, then finely grate the zests. Take the pears out of the soaking water and if they have softened, squeeze out and finely dice. If they are still hard, return them to the soaking water, bring to the boil , turn off the heat and leave in the hot water for about 5 minutes, leave to cool briefly, then chop. Reserve about 200 ml of the soaking water.

5 Add all the fruits, the hazelnuts, all the spices, the orange and the lemon zest to the dough in the bowl, briefly knead through to combine. Transfer the dough to a floured work surface and knead again with your hands to combine well. Divide the dough into 5 even-sized portions and shape each one into a smooth oval loaf.

6 Line two baking trays with baking paper. Place the loaves with sufficent space next to each other onto the trays. Brush the tops of the fruit loaves with a little of the reserved soaking liquid, cover and leave to rise for 1 hour in a warm place.

7 Preheat the oven to 175°C (convection is best; see tips). Put the baking trays with the loaves into the oven (one tray at the top, the other one at the bottom). Bake the loaves for about 1 hour, brushing the tops again all over with the reserved soaking water after 30 minutes and after 45 minutes. Take the finished Christmas fruit breads out of the oven, place them on a cooling rack and brush again several times with the soaking water. Leave to cool.

8 To serve, cut the fruit breads into thin slices and place them on a platter or a large cake plate. The bread tastes great with butter – put some butter on the table so that everyone can spread their slices to their hearts' content.

USEFUL TIPS

Making the Christmas fruit bread is time-consuming, and so it is definitely worth making several loaves at the same time. The fruit bread will also keep very well – store it wrapped in aluminium foil in the fridge for several weeks.

The use of convection heat is recommended for baking the fruit breads because it allows you to put all the breads into the oven at the same time. If you can only set your oven to top and bottom heat, make sure you preheat it to 195°C and bake the breads one at a time in the centre of the oven as described.

GINGERBREADS

Here in Bavaria, these aromatic flat pastries are a traditional baked treat before Christmas – sometimes they are made with a dark glaze, sometimes with sugar icing, sometimes they are served plain. And if you like, you can decorate the gingerbreads with a couple of almond halves or, for special occasions, cover them elegantly with gold leaf or gold powder.

AN ABSOLUTE MUST

MAKES ABOUT 16 GINGERBREADS:

For the gingerbreads:
2 egg whites (medium)
a pinch of salt
150 g sugar
½ tsp hartshorn (c. 3 g)
100 g ground skinned almonds
50 g ground hazelnuts
40 g nutty nougat
30 g each candied lemon and orange peel
100 g raw marzipan
1 heaped tbsp quince jelly (c. 25 g)
1 tsp gingerbread spice mix
½ tsp cocoa powder
1 level tbsp cornflour (c. 10 g)
½ each organic orange and lemon
c. 16 rice paper discs (7 cm diameter)

For the garnish:
400 g dark cooking chocolate (see tips)
if liked, 2 leaves edible gold leaf (23.75 carat) or gold powder (see right)

Plus:
baking paper | soufflé dish (c. 7 cm diameter)

HOW LONG IT TAKES: c. 40 min
DRYING: c. 12 hours
IN THE OVEN: c. 12 min
PER GINGERBREAD: c. 290 kcal | 4 g p | 16 g f | 32 g ch

1 Put the egg whites and the salt into the bowl of a food processor (or work with a mixing bowl and a handheld mixer). Beat for about 7 minutes with the whisks until you have a creamy stiff eggwhite mixture, gradually sprinkling in the sugar while you are whisking. Put the hartshorn into a cup with 1 teaspoon of lukewarm water and stir to dissolve. Then add to the egg white mixture and whisk for another 2 minutes.

2 Meanwhile, dry-roast the almonds and the hazelnuts in a frying pan without fat until golden, take out. Cut the nougat into small pieces and melt in a bowl over a hot waterbath. Finely chop the candied fruits in an electric blender or with a knife. Break the marzipan into small pieces and stir into the quince jelly. Combine the gingerbread spice mix, cocoa and cornflour. Wash the lemon and the orange under hot water and pat dry, finely grate the zests.

3 Combine the marzipan mixture with the nougat and 2 tablespoons of the egg white mixture, then fold it into the rest of the egg white mixture together with all the other ingredients. Now place the gingerbread mixture, a tablespoon at a time, on top of the rice paper discs (about 35 g per disc). Place the discs onto an upside down soufflé dish. Using a smooth-bladed knife spread the gingerbread mixture in a dome shape over the discs (or use a gingerbread bell, see tip). Place the gingerbreads side by side on a large wooden board and leave to dry for about 12 hours (or better overnight).

4 The next day, preheat the oven to 175°C (use top and bottom heat, convection is not recommended). Line a baking tray with baking paper and place the gingerbreads on top, with a little space in between. Bake in the oven (centre) for about 12 minutes. Take out of the oven and place on a rack to cool.

5 Roughly chop the dark chocolate. Put two-thirds into a metal bowl and melt over a hot waterbath. Gradually stir in the remaining chocolate and melt. To check that the chocolate is ready to use, either dip the tip of a knife into the molten chocolate mixture – it should set quite quickly and be glossy. Or dunk a wooden spoon into the chocolate and take it to your lips – it should feel cool.

6 Now dip the gingerbreads headfirst into the chocolate mixture, leave the surplus to drip off, then turn over and place onto the cooling rack. Allow the chocolate coating to set. If liked, just before the chocolate coating has set completely, decorate the gingerbreads with a little leaf gold or gold powder.

USEFUL TIPS

It's particularly easy to spread the gingerbread mixture on top of the rice paper discs if you use a special gingerbread bell (see picture top left). These utensils are available in Bavarian household stores.
Melt more chocolate for the coating than you will need. This makes it easier to dip the gingerbreads in the mixture. Allow any leftover chocolate to cool and melt again as and when needed. If you find preparing the chocolate a little challenging you can use a ready-made cake glaze instead.
The gingerbreads should mature for at least 10 days in an air-tight container before you try them. They will get better and moister during this time.

LOVELY AND GOLDEN

Edible gold leaf and gold powder are easy to order on the Internet or from an artists' supply shop. Gold leaf is applied using a dry, soft make-up brush. Rub the brush a little against your skin to give it a static charge, then use it to take a little gold leaf off the paper and jazz up the gingerbreads (pictured above).

SWEET 7TH HEAVEN

... is where Bavaria's top treats will take you. Whether it be a doughnut in the morning, a cream puff in the afternoon or a raspberry cream in the evening – you've got to have something sweet.

PLUM TART

Opinions are divided over whether it should be baked on a tray or in a springform, with shortcrust pastry or yeast dough, with or without crumble, with cinnamon or not. Everyone has their favourite, but one thing they're all agreed on: even raw, the plums need to be juicy and full of flavour.

FRUITY AND SWEET

MAKES 1 SPRINGFORM (28 cm diameter, c. 12 pieces):

For the dough:

250 g flour | 60 g icing sugar
125 g soft butter | 2 egg yolks (medium)
a pinch of finely grated organic lemon zest
a dash of rum | a pinch of salt
½ vanilla pod
flour for rolling out | butter for the dish

For the topping:

1 kg plums
4 sponge fingers or shortbreads (c. 35 g)
1 tbsp sugar | a pinch of ground cinnamon

HOW LONG IT TAKES: c. 30 min
CHILLING: c. 2 hours
IN THE OVEN: c. 1 hour
PER PIECE: c. 245 kcal | 4 g p | 11 g f | 32 g ch

1 To make the dough, sift the flour and the icing sugar onto the work surface, make a well in the centre. Put the butter in pats into the hollow, together with the egg yolks, lemon zest, rum and salt. Slit the vanilla pod open lengthways and scrape out the seeds, then add to the flour. Now quickly combine everything with your fingers, rubbing it between your hands until you have a homogenous mixture that you can knead into a dough. Press the dough flat with your hands and shape it into a rectangle, then wrap it in clingfilm and chill it in the fridge for at least 2 hours.

2 To prepare the topping, wash and pat dry the plums. To remove the stones, cut the plums lengthways on one side, making a short crossways cut at the ends so you have a cross. Split the plums open along the long cut and remove the stone. Break the sponge fingers or shortbread into chunks, put them into a tall mixing container and process to small crumbs with a handheld blender. Combine the sugar with the cinnamon.

3 Preheat the oven to 175°C, lightly grease the springform with butter. Roll out the dough on the floured work surface to about c. ½ cm thick, turning it frequently and dusting with more flour. Cut a circle the size of the springform out of the dough and carefully transfer it to the base of the pan. Knead the remaining dough together, then roll it out as a long ribbon (about 4 cm wide) and roll it up. Use to line the sides of the springform, press so it adheres well.

4 Spread the biscuit crumbs evenly over the dough base and cover densely with plums. Start at the outside, arranging the plums all round tightly next to each other so that the tips stand up nicely. Sprinkle with the cinnamon sugar. Bake the plum tart in the oven (centre, convection 155°C) for 50–60 minutes. Take the plum tart out, leave to cool to lukewarm and loosen out of the springform. Tastes best served immediately with a dollop of whipped cream.

BAVARIAN DOUGHNUTS

Whatever they're called – Auszogne, Striezel, Schmalznudeln, Krapfen or Kiacherl – they're all made with yeast dough and deep-fried in clarified butter. These doughnuts are pinched before baking which gives them their characteristic shape.

BAVARIAN AND DEEP-FRIED

MAKES C. 12 DOUGHNUTS:

For the dough:
¼ l milk | 30 g fresh yeast
550 g flour | 50 g sugar
a pinch of salt | 100 g butter
2 eggs (medium) | 1 egg yolk (medium)
100 g raisins | 2 tbsp rum
flour for working
1 kg clarified butter for deep-frying

For coating:
80 g sugar
1 heaped tbsp vanilla sugar (see tip, p.135)

HOW LONG IT TAKES: c. 1 hour
RESTING: c. 1 hour 45 min
PER DOUGHNUT: c. 385 kcal | 8 g p | 16 g f | 52 g ch

1 To make the dough, heat the milk to lukewarm. Crumble the yeast into a cup, then stir it together with 4 tablespoons of milk, 1 teaspoon of flour and 2 teaspoons of sugar. Put the remaining flour into the bowl of a food processor (or work with a mixing bowl and a handheld mixer) and make a hollow in the middle. Sprinkle the sides all round with the remaining sugar and the salt. Pour the yeast mixture into the hollow, cover the mixture with a cloth and leave to rest in a warm place for 15 minutes.

2 Cut the butter into large chunks, then add these with the eggs and the egg yolk to the remaining milk (do not stir). Drizzle the raisins with the rum.

3 Add the egg-butter-milk mixture to the flour mixture and knead for 5 minutes with kneading hooks until you have a smooth dough. Briefly knead the dough again with your hands on a floured work surface, then return it to the floured bowl, cover and leave to rest for 45 minutes.

4 Add the soaked raisins to the dough and knead again with the kneading hooks. On the floured work surface, roll the dough to a longish rope and divide it into 12 even-sized pieces. Shape the pieces into smooth balls and place on a floured baking tray with sufficient space in between. Cover the dough balls and leave to rest for 45 minutes.

5 In a large, wide saucepan, heat the clarified butter to about 160°C. The fat has reached the right temperature when you hold the handle of a wooden spoon into the fat and bubbles rise immediately. In a deep plate, combine sugar and vanilla sugar for coating.

6 Using scissors, cut a cross into the tops of the risen dough balls. Place 4 doughnuts with the cut side down into the hot fat, cover and deep-fry for 2 minutes. Turn the doughnuts (careful, the grease may splatter!) and deep-fry for about 5 minutes without lid until golden brown, turning them once more. Lift out and briefly drain on kitchen paper, then turn to coat in the vanilla sugar while still hot. Cook the remaining doughnuts as described. Leave to cool to lukewarm or completely and serve.

APPLE TRAYBAKE

Apple varieties like Braeburn or Pink Lady are particularly well suited for baking. Highly aromatic, these apples are slightly tart in flavour and virtually "collapse" onto the dough when baked. They are also excellent storage apples.

CLASSIC AND GOOD

MAKES 1 BAKING TRAY (32 x 40 cm, c. 12 pieces):

For the dough:

600 g flour
250 g icing sugar
375 g soft butter
2 eggs (medium)
a pinch of salt
1 vanilla pod
flour for working

For the topping:

1.5 kg tart apples (e.g. Braeburn)
3 tbsp brown sugar
4 tbsp rum (just leave it out if children are among your guests)
freshly squeezed juice of ½ lemon

For brushing:

1 egg yolk (medium) | 2 tbsp milk

HOW LONG IT TAKES: c. 35 min
CHILLING: c. 2 hours
IN THE OVEN: c. 1 hour
PER PIECE: c. 585 kcal | 7 g p | 29 g f | 71 g ch

1 To make the dough, sift the flour and the icing sugar onto the work surface, make a hollow in the middle. Put the butter in pats together with the eggs into the hollow. Slit the vanilla pod lengthways, scrape out the seeds and add. Now, working from the outside, combine everything quickly with your fingers, rubbing it between your hands, until you have a mixture that you can knead into a smooth dough. Press the dough with your hands to flatten, halve and shape into two rectangles. Cover with clingfilm and chill for at least 2 hours.

2 To prepare the topping, peel and quarter the apples, remove the cores, cut into 1½ cm wedges. Put the apple wedges into a bowl with the sugar, rum and lemon juice and leave to marinate. Combine the egg yolk and the milk for brushing.

3 Preheat the oven to 175°C, line the baking tray with baking paper. Roll out one of the dough halves on the floured work surface to about 3 mm thick and the size of the baking tray, turning it frequently and dusting it with flour. Carefully roll the dough base from the narrow side onto a rolling pin, then slowly unroll it again onto the baking tray. Prick the dough base several times with a fork.

4 Place the apples closely packed onto the dough base. Roll out the second dough half as described above and use to cover the apples. Press the edges together all round and use a fork to reshape. Prick the dough cover several times with a fork, then brush it with the beaten egg yolk.

5 Put the tray into the oven (centre, convection 155°C) and bake the tart for about 1 hour until golden. Take the tart out, leave to cool to lukewarm, divide into large pieces and serve.

Oktoberfest

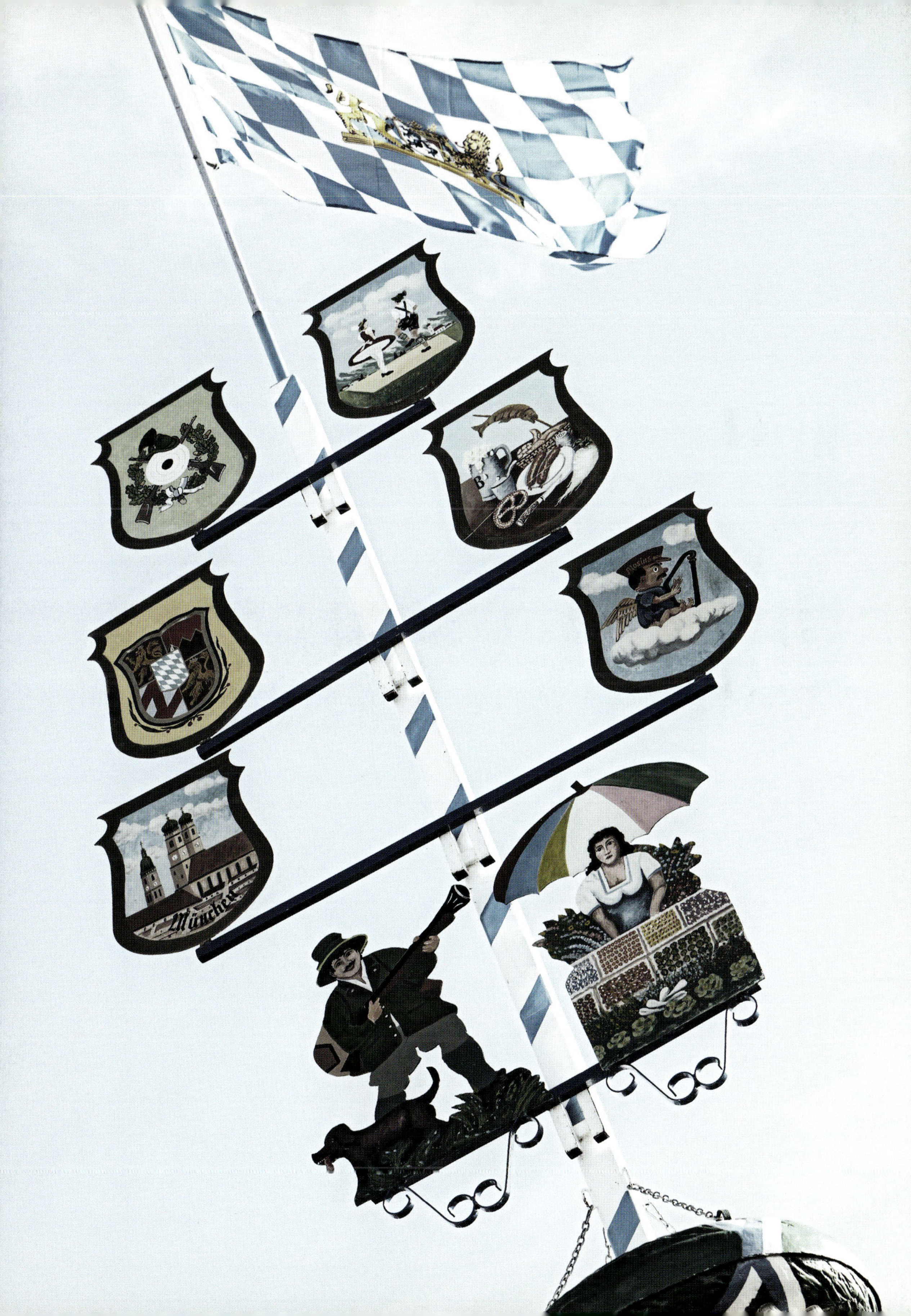
München

BAVARIAN CHEESECAKE

Bavarian cheesecake is not like any other cheesecake! The secret lies in the combination of ingredients and of course in the method of preparation – the cake should be light and smooth after baking, and should definitely not stick to the palate.

TOO GOOD TO EAT

MAKES 1 SPRINGFORM (28 cm diameter, c. 12 pieces):

For the dough:

100 g flour | 1½ tbsp icing sugar (c. 30 g)
50 g soft butter | 1 egg yolk (medium)
a pinch of finely grated zest of organic lemon
a pinch of salt
flour for working | butter for the dish

For the topping:

750 g low-fat quark
3 eggs (medium) | 3 egg yolks (medium)
200 ml milk | a pinch of salt
finely grated zest and 2 tbsp freshly squeezed juice of ½ organic lemon
seeds of ½ vanilla pod
150 g sugar | 90 g cornflour
50 g butter | 200 g cream
icing sugar for dusting

HOW LONG IT TAKES: c. 35 min
CHILLING: c. 1 hour
IN THE OVEN: c. 1 hour 30 min
PER PIECE: c. 340 kcal | 13 g p | 17 g f | 33 g ch

1 To make the dough, sift the flour and the icing sugar onto a floured work surface and make a hollow in the middle. Put the butter in pats into the hollow with the egg yolk, lemon zest and salt. Now combine everything with your fingers, rubbing it between your hands until you can knead it to a smooth dough. Press the dough to flatten, wrap in clingfilm and chill for at least 1 hour.

2 Preheat the oven to 180°C (use top and bottom heat, convection is not recommended), and line a baking tray with baking paper. On the floured work surface, roll out the dough about 2–3 mm thick, turning it repeatedly and dusting with flour. Place the springform on top of the dough and cut all around, setting the cut-off dough aside. Place the dough circle onto the baking tray and bake in the oven (centre) for about 10 minutes until golden, then take out and leave to cool.

3 Meanwhile prepare the topping. Using a whisk, stir the quark with the eggs, egg yolks, milk, salt, lemon zest and juice as well as the vanilla seeds. Combine 140 g sugar and the cornflour, then gradually whisk into the quark mixture. Melt the butter and slowly whisk into the mixture. Beat the cream until stiff, then fold in.

4 Separate and lightly grease the springform base and sides with butter. Place the baked pastry base onto the base of the form, then put the sides onto the form base and tighten. Fill the gap between pastry base and form sides with the reserved raw dough mixture. Put the quark mixture on the pastry base, sprinkle with the remaining sugar.

5 Reduce the oven temperature to 175°C. Bake the cheesecake in the oven (centre) for 1 hour 30 minutes until golden. Using a knife, loosen the edge after about 35 minutes. If the top turns too dark, cover with aluminium foil. Remove from the oven, leave to cool, dust with icing sugar and take out of the form.

MARBLED GUGLHUPF

The secret of a gugelhupf lies in its beautiful marbling. It's the only way to guarantee a perfect mixture of light and dark dough in every single piece.

BLACK AND WHITE, NOT WHITE AND BLUE

MAKES 1 GUGELHUPF (24 cm diameter and c. 1.5 l volume, c. 12 pieces):

100 g dark cooking chocolate
1 tsp sunflower oil
150 g flour
150 g cornflour
1 tsp baking powder
250 g icing sugar
200 g soft butter
a pinch of salt
seeds of 1 vanilla pod
finely grated zest of ½ organic lemon
6 eggs (medium) at room temperature
icing sugar for dusting
butter and flour for the dish

HOW LONG IT TAKES: c. 35 min
IN THE OVEN: c. 1 hour
PER PIECE: c. 395 kcal | 6 g p | 21 g f | 45 g ch

1 Finely chop the chocolate, place it in a metal bowl and melt over a hot waterbath. Stir in the oil and leave to cool to lukewarm.

2 Preheat the oven to 175°C. Thinly but thoroughly grease a gugelhupf pan with butter, then evenly dust with flour, shaking out any surplus flour. Combine the flour with the cornfour and the baking powder.

3 Put the icing sugar with the butter and the salt into the bowl of a food processor (or work with a mxing bowl and a handheld mixer), then beat with the whisks for 5 minutes until light and creamy. Add the vanilla seeds, lemon zest and 1 egg and stir well to combine. Now beat the mixture for another 6–7 minutes, gradually adding the remaining eggs. Lastly, whisk in the flour mixture on a low speed.

4 Take about 300 g of the mixture and put it into a second bowl. Stir in the lukewarm chocolate. Put one-third of the vanilla mixture into the gugelhupf pan, then spread half the chocolate mixture on top. Add the second third of the vanilla mixture, spread the remaining chocolate mixture on top, finish with the remaining vanilla mixture. Push a two-pronged fork into the dough, then carefully pull it in a slow, circular motion from bottom to top through the entire mixture. Repeat the process, creating the beautiful marbling of the cake.

5 Bake the gugelhopf in the oven (centre, convection 155°C) for about 1 hour. If the top gets too dark, cover with aluminium foil. The cake is done if a thin wooden skewer comes out clean when you push it into the cake. Take the cake out of the oven, leave to cool for 10 minutes, then tip it onto a cake grid and thickly dust with icing sugar while still hot. Leave the cake to cool completely, divide into pieces and serve.

CREAM HURRICANES WITH CHERRIES

Bavarians like to exaggerate a bit and they also like to have plenty on their plates, so a cream puff just won't do – it simply has to be a cream hurricane.

HEAVENLY SWEET

MAKES C. 4 PIECES:

For the dough:

70 g flour | a pinch of baking powder
120 ml milk | 1½ tbsp butter (c. 30 g)
a pinch of salt | 2 eggs (medium)

For the filling:

1 jar morello cherries (volume 680 g)
½ vanilla pod | 2 tbsp brown sugar
2 pieces organic orange zest (c. 5 cm each)
a pinch of ground cinnamon | 3 tsp cornflour
1 tbsp kirsch | 600 g cream
2 tsp vanilla sugar (see tip, p.135)

Plus:

icing sugar for dusting
piping bag with a star nozzle (c. 13 mm diameter)

HOW LONG IT TAKES: c. 45 min
IN THE OVEN: c. 20 min
PER SERVING: c. 745 kcal | 10 g p | 58 g f | 42 g ch

1 Preheat the oven to 220°C (convection 200°C), line a baking tray with baking paper. To make the dough, combine the flour and the baking powder. In a saucepan, bring the milk, butter and salt to the boil. Add the flour, stir in with a wooden spoon until the dough comes away from the side, forms a ball, and a white coating appears on the base of the pan.

2 Put the dough into a bowl and briefly leave to cool. Then stir in the eggs, one at a time, with the whisks of a handheld mixer until you have a glossy, smooth choux pastry. Transfer the pastry into a piping bag with a star nozzle.

3 Pipe the choux pastry onto the baking tray as 4 flat rosettes (c. 7 cm diameter), leaving plenty of space between them. Put the tray into the oven (centre), pour a generous dash of water into the bottom of the oven and immediately close the oven door. Bake the cream hurricanes for 18–20 minutes until golden. Immediately clean the piping bag and the nozzle and stand them up to dry. Take the cream hurricanes out of the oven and place them on a cake grid to cool completely.

4 Meanwhile, make the filling. Drain the cherries in a sieve, catching the juice. Slit the vanilla pod open lengthways and scrape out the seeds. Melt the sugar in a saucepan over medium heat for 3 minutes until caramelized to light brown. Pour in the cherry juice and bring to the boil. Add the vanilla pod and the seeds, the orange zest and the cinnamon and cook for 5 minutes. Stir the cornflour into 2–3 tablespoons of cold water, add to the juice, cook for 3 minutes, stirring constantly. Lastly, stir in the kirsch and the cherries, take off the heat and leave to cool.

5 Halve the cream hurricanes crossways, put the cherries onto the lower halves. Beat the cream with the vanilla sugar until stiff and put it into the piping bag. Pipe the cream as giant rosettes onto the cherries, cover with the cream hurricane lids. Dust with plenty of icing sugar and serve.

USEFUL TIP

Placing water into the bottom of the oven creates steam inside which makes the dough rise beautifully so do not open the oven door while baking!

SWEET BAVARIA!

Most people associate Bavaria with hearty dishes like white sausages and pretzels, roast pork with dumplings, or freshly smoked whitefish with a nice cold beer. But the family ties between the Bavarian Wittelsbach and the Austrian Habsburg dynasties mean that there is also a wide range of exquisite sweet pastries, desserts and cakes.

With dairy farms in the mountains and the valleys, there was always enough milk for "Schmalznudeln" (doughnut cakes), "Zwetschgendatschi" (plum cakes) or sugary, golden "Auszogne" (Bavarian fritters) – a popular speciality which the farmer's wives would prepare during harvest time and major festivities such as parish fairs. On specific holidays and feast days, there would also be traditional and uniquely shaped bakery items, such as "Allerseelenzopf" (All Saints' braided yeast bread), "Osterlamm" (Easter lamb-shaped cake) and "Lebkuchen" (gingerbread). Today, flavoursome Hefezöpfe (a type of braided bread) with a bit of butter and homemade jam are perfect for breakfast or with an afternoon coffee. Some of the cakes are also suitable as sweet main meals. In Catholic Bavaria, for example, apple or elderflower pancakes would often be served on a Friday, when no meat was eaten.

A LITTLE TIPPLE FOR GOOD MEASURE

It is not just after a hearty meal that connoisseurs enjoy a flavoursome fruit brandy, which has been made using fruits from meadow orchards filled with blackthorn, apple, cherry and plum trees since time immemorial. This fruit-growing business, which many small-scale farmers have been perpetuating for generations, was and is typical of the hilly upland region here. While farmers primarily concentrated on the dairy industry, they also grew fruit on the otherwise hard-to-tend slopes as a source of additional income, as well as for the family's fruit stores and preserves. Many old fruit varieties and their typically intense flavours have thus been preserved in these meadow orchards as a result of their exceptional robustness. Flavours and choice of fruit are what ultimately define a fruit brandy, which warms the heart after a good solid meal, but particularly settles the stomach.

Classic fruit brandy is distilled from apples and pears, and is among the most popular. Pear schnapps, also known as "Willi", after the Williams pear, is one of the most intensely aromatic brandies, and the typical regional pears from trees often over a hundred years old are a real speciality. Plum brandy also has a distinct taste. Some distillers leave their damson plums to ripen on the tree until late autumn, when the fruits have wizened up, enabling a "sweet late vintage" of sorts. The cherries used in kirsch, meanwhile, have things a little tougher in the rainy foothills of the Alps. Yet this cherry brandy is the pride of every distiller. Others made from mirabelle plums, greengage, quince, rowan berries (from the rowan tree), sloes (from blackthorn bushes), cornelian cherries and elderberries perfectly round off the wide range of ancient Bavarian brandies.

APPLE FRITTERS WITH VANILLA CUSTARD

Apple fritters are traditionally deep-fried in batter, which is of course what we'll do here. After cooking, they should be nicely "puffed" and crisp – and should not sit around for too long. Best to eat them straightaway then!

NO WORDS ... JUST YUM!

SERVES 4–6 (c. 20 pieces):

For the custard:

1 vanilla pod | ½ l milk
5 egg yolks (medium) | 2 heaped tbsp sugar (c. 40 g)
a pinch of ground cinnamon

For the cinnamon sugar:

100 g sugar | 1 tsp ground cinnamon
½ tsp vanilla sugar (see tip, p.135)

For the fritters:

500 g deep-frying fat
2 tbsp butter | 2 eggs (medium)
150 ml beer (lager)
140 g flour | a good pinch of baking powder
a pinch of salt | 1 tsp sugar
4 large tart apples (e.g. Granny Smith)
freshly squeezed juice of ½ lemon

Plus: apple corer

HOW LONG IT TAKES: c. 45 min
IN THE OVEN: c. 20 min
PER FRITTER: c. 170 kcal | 3 g p | 10 g f | 16 g ch

1 To make the custard, slit the vanilla pod lengthways and scrape out the seeds. Put the milk, vanilla pod and seeds into a saucepan and heat. In a metal bowl (with a rounded base), combine the egg yolks with the sugar and the cinnamon, adding the vanilla milk gradually through a sieve. Heat the milk over a hot waterbath for about 10 minutes, stirring constantly, until you have a thick, creamy custard. Place the bowl into iced water and let the custard cool, stirring frequently so no skin forms.

2 To make the cinnamon sugar, put all the ingredients into a deep plate and stir to combine, then set aside. Heat the deep-frying fat in a small, tall saucepan (160–170°C, bubbles should appear immediately when dipping the handle of a wooden spoon into the fat).

3 To make the fritters, melt the butter. Separate the eggs. Lightly beat the egg yolks with a whisk. Add the beer, flour and baking powder and stir until smooth. Drizzle in the butter. Whisk the egg whites with salt and sugar until stiff. Carefully fold into the batter.

4 Peel the apples, remove the cores with an apple corer and cut each apple into 1 cm slices. Drizzle the apple rings with lemon juice. Dunk 4 apple rings completely into the batter, lift out with a fork, scraping off a little of the batter. Put the apple rings into the hot fat, deep-fry for 2–3 minutes, turn (see tips) and deep-fry for another 2 minutes until golden. Using a slotted spoon, lift the fritters out of the fat, drain them briefly on kitchen paper and turn them in the cinnamon sugar to coat, shaking off any excess. Prepare the remaining apple slices in the same way. Serve with the vanilla custard.

USEFUL TIPS

When deep-frying, the apple fritters are ready to be turned as soon as you can see a golden brown edge all around.

If you're making larger quantities, you can also keep the fritters warm in the oven at 120°C for a short while. Not too long – or they'll collapse.

TIPSY CREAM WITH RASPBERRIES

A little shot of brandy at the end of a meal is always permitted. You won't need it however when you enjoy this lovely cream – it's full of spirit in its own right. A dessert for grown-ups. Cheers!

SWEET AND BOOZY

SERVES 4:

For the cream:

1 piece dark chocolate (c. 30 g)
200 g white chocolate
2 leaves gelatine
200 g fresh raspberries
2 eggs (medium) | 1 tsp sugar
300 g cream
3 cl framboise (raspberry eau de vie, optional)
some light or dark chocolate flakes (optional)

For the sauce:

300 g frozen raspberries
a dash of freshly squeezed lemon juice
1 tbsp icing sugar
1 tsp framboise (raspberry eau de vie, otional)
Plus: fine kitchen brush

HOW LONG IT TAKES: c. 50 min
CHILLING: c. 4 hours
PER SERVING: c. 670 kcal | 11 g p | 49 g f | 42 g ch

1 Finely chop the dark chocolate, put it into a metal bowl and melt it over a hot waterbath. Dunk the brush into the chocolate and "paint" the insides of 4 tall glasses with it.

2 Finely chop the white chocolate and melt two-thirds of it over a hot waterbath. Take off the stove and stir in the remaining chopped chocolate, then leave to cool. Place the gelatine leaves in cold water so they are completely covered, and soak for about 5–10 minutes.

3 Pick over the fresh raspberries and reserve 12, then halve the remaining berries. Separate the eggs. Beat the egg whites and the sugar with the whisks of a handheld mixer until stiff. Beat the cream, but not too stiff. Beat the egg yolks for 2–3 minutes until creamy, then stir in the lukewarm white chocolate. Stir in one-third of the beaten egg whites, add a little cream and mix in with a spatula. Fold in the remaining beaten egg whites and again a little cream with a spatula.

4 Lightly squeeze the gelatine and put into a small saucepan. Melt over medium heat, stir in 2 tablespoons of cream. Combine the gelatine mixture with the remaining cream. Now gently fold the mixture into the chocolate cream. Lastly, stir in the framboise if liked and fold in the halved raspberries. Transfer the cream into the prepared glasses, cover with clingfilm and chill for at least 4 hours (better overnight).

5 To make the sauce, thaw the frozen raspberries. Put them into a tall mixing container together with the lemon juice and the icing sugar and finely purée with a handheld blender. If liked, stir in the framboise. Push the fruit purée through a fine sieve to remove any seeds.

6 Take the glasses out of the fridge. Garnish the cream with the reserved raspberries and chocolate flakes if using. Serve with the raspberry sauce.

EASY CONVERSIONS

Dry Measurements

METRIC	UK	US - FLOUR	US – SUGAR, BUTTER
7g	¼oz		
15g	½oz	⅛ cup	
25g	1oz		
30g		¼ cup	⅛ cup
40g	1 ½oz	⅓ cup	
50g	2oz		
55g			¼ cup
60g	2 ½oz	½ cup	
70g		⅝ cup	
75g	3oz	⅔ cup	⅓ cup
85g		¾ cup	
90g	3 ½oz		
100g	4oz	⅞ cup	
110g		1 cup	
115g			½ cup
140g			⅝ cup
150g	5oz		⅔ cup
165g	5 ½oz		
170g			¾ cup
175g	6oz		
200g	7oz		⅞ cup
215g	7 ½oz		
225g	8oz		1 cup
250g	9oz		
275g	10oz		
325g	11oz		
350g	12oz		
375g	13oz		
400g	14oz		
450g	1lb		
500g	1lb 2oz		
575g	1 ¼lb		
700g	1 ½lb		
800g	1 ¾lb		
900g	2lb		
1kg	2 ¼lb		
1.5kg	3 ½lb		

Liquid Measurements

METRIC	UK	US
45 ml	1 ½ fl oz	
60 ml	2 fl oz	⅛ cup
75 ml	2 ½ fl oz	
90 ml	3 fl oz	¼ cup
115 ml		⅓ cup
125 ml	4 fl oz	
150 ml	¼ pint, 5 fl oz	
175 ml	6 fl oz	½ cup
200 ml	7 fl oz	⅝ cup
225 ml	8 fl oz	⅔ cup
230 ml		¾ cup
250 ml	9 fl oz	
300 ml	½ pint, 10 fl oz	⅞ cup
315 ml		1 cup
350 ml		
375 ml	12 fl oz	
390 ml		
415 ml		
425 ml	14 fl oz	
450 ml	¾ pint, 15 fl oz	
475 ml	16 fl oz	
500 ml	18 fl oz	
530 ml		
550 ml		
600 ml	1 pint, 20 fl oz	
630 ml		
650 ml		
715 ml		
750 ml	1 ¼ pint	
900 ml	1 ½ pint, 30 fl oz	
950 ml		
1 litre	1 ¾ pint	
1.2 litres	2 pint	
1.5 litres	2 ½ pint	
1.7 litres	3 pint	
2 litres	3 ¼ pint	
2.4 litres	4 pint	
3 litres	5 pint	

Oven Temperatures

CENTIGRADE	FAHRENHEIT	GAS
110	225	¼ (104 C/220 F)
130	250	½
140	275	1
150	300	2
170	325	3
180	350	4
190	375	5
200	400	6
220	425	7
230	450	8
240	475	9

Sizes

METRIC	UK/US
3 mm	⅛ in
6 mm	¼ in
8 mm	⅓ in
1 cm	½ in
2 cm	¾ in
2.5 cm	1 in
3 cm	1 ½ in
5 cm	2 in
6 cm	2 ½ in
7.5 cm	3 in
9 cm	3 ½ in
10 cm	4 in
11.5 cm	4 ½ in
12.5 cm	5 in
15 cm	6 in
18 cm	7 in
19 cm	7 ½ in
20 cm	8 in
23 cm	9 in
24 cm	9 ½ in
25 cm	10 in
27 cm	11 in
30 cm	12 in
33 cm	13 in
38 cm	15 in
40 cm	16 in

BAVARIAN INTERPRETER

To help you find your way around, order a beer and a meal, and make contact with fellow beer drinkers at the Oktoberfest, we're here giving you a basic understanding of the most common Bavarian expressions, from greetings and salutations to putting the world to rights – so you'll never be lost for words.

A

Antn, Bauernantn	duck, farmyard duck
Apfekiacherl	deep-fried apple slices in a beer batter, apple fritters
Apfekuacha	apple tart, apple pie
Arme Ritter	poor knights, a dessert made from old bread rolls
Auszogne	deep-fried yeast pastry, fritter or doughnut

B

Bauchstecherl	finger-shaped potato dumplings or gnocchi
Bia	beer
Blutwurscht	black pudding
Bittsche(n)!	There you are!
Blaukraut	red cabbage
boarisch	Bavarian
Brezn	pretzels
Brotzeitkörberl	Brotzeit basket
Bua, Buam	boy, young man
busseln	kissing

D

Dampfnudln	yeast dumplings
Dankschе(n)!	Thank you!
Dirndl	girl, also: traditional costume for women in Bavaria
Dschuidigung!	Sorry!

E/F

Fleischpflanzerl	burger

G

Gamsbart	Bavarian hat decoration made from the hair of the male chamois goat-antelope's lower neck
Ganserl	goose
Gaudi	fun
Gmias	vegetables
a gmischter Salod	a mixed salad
Grachal	lemonade
Griebenschmalz/ Grammeschmoiz	a pork dripping spread with spices and onions
Grießnockerl	dumplings/gnocchi made from a semolina mixture with eggs and butter
Gröstl	a hearty fry-up with meat and potato leftovers from the previous day
gschmorts Reh-schäuferl	braised shoulder of venison
Guglhupf	a ring cake or Bundt cake

H

a Haferl Kaffee	a large mug of coffee
Haxn, Schweinshaxn	pork knuckle (in Bavaria it's always fried, never boiled)
Hendl/Giggal	roast chicken
Hollerkiacherl	doughnut with elderflowers

I/J

jodeln	yodelling, a special singing technique in the Alps

K

Kalbsbries	veal sweetbreads
Kalbsnierenbraten	pot-roast belly of veal with kidney stuffing
Kartoffelbrei	potato purée
Kas	cheese
Kaskuacha	Bavarian cheesecake
Kini	king
Kirchweihganserl	St Martin's goose
Knödel	dumpling(s)
Kraut	cabbage
Krautwickerl	stuffed cabbage leaf/leaves
Krusterl	crust, e.g. crackling of a pork roast or on yeast dumplings
Kuacha	cake

L

Laugenstangerl	pretzel breadsticks
Leberknödelsuppn	liver dumpling soup
an Lidda	a litre

M/N

Madl	girl
Mannsbuid	man
Marmelad	jam
a Maß Bier	1 litre of beer in a stein
Milli	milk
Moizbier	malted beer

O

Obazda	a spiced cheese spread with onions
Obstler	fruit brandy
Ochsenbackerl	ox cheeks
Ois klar?	Everything ok?
Orkanbeutel	large cream puff(s)

P

Pfannakuacha	pancake/omelette
Pfennigmuckerl	type of bread roll
Pflanzerl	burger
Presssack	boiled sausage of pork and pig skin

R

Radi	Bavarian beer radish
Radieserl	radish
Radla, Ruß	a drink of half lemonade and half light beer or wheat beer, shandy
Reherl	chanterelle mushrooms
Reiberdatschi	potato pancake
Rindsbriah	beef broth

S/T

Saftl, Natursaftl	juice, meat stock
Salod	salad
Schmankerl	delicious dish, delicacy, dessert
Schmarrn	a sweet pastry consisting of a thick pancake, torn into pieces; hearty also with potatoes or dumplings; also means: rubbish, nonsense

Schupfnudeln	finger gnocchi
Schwammerl	mushrooms
Schweinsbratn	pork roast
Semmeln	bread rolls
Spatzn	spaetzle
Spofaki	suckling pig
Stamperl	shot glass (2 cl)
Steckerlfisch	fish kebab
Sterz	a simple dish made from porridge or potatoes
Strammer Max	fried bread covered with fried egg and ham
Sulz, Tellersulz	brawn, head cheese
Suppn	soup

W

Wirsching	Savoy cabbage
Wos?	What?
Wuid	game
Wurschtsalod	sausage slices with a vinegar and oil dressing, sausage salad
Wurschtradel	slice(s) of sausage or cold meat

Z

Zwetschgendatschi	plum cake (usually from the tray)
Zwickte	yeast pastry, snipped on top with scissors and then deep-fried in clarified butter

AT THE TAVERN

Hock di hera, dann samma mera!	Sit down here and there'll be more of us. Join us.
Hobt's an Durscht?	Are you thirsty?
Hobt's an Hunga?	Are you hungry?
Wos derfs sei? Wos griangs'n?	What can I get you?
Megt's wos Z'dringa und wos Z'essen?	Would you like something to drink and eat?
Wos gibt'sn heid Middog?	What do you have for lunch today?
I mechad aa a Bia.	I'd also like a beer (please).
I griag no oane.	Another beer, please.
Oane gäd awei no!	I'll have one more!
Ozapft is!	The barrel has been tapped and the beer is flowing liberally.
a frisch zapfte Maß	a beer fresh from the barrel
Oans, zwoa, gsuffa!	One, two, bottoms up!
Prost mitanand!	Cheers! To your health!
An Guadn!	Bon appetit!
I kon nimma.	I can't have any more. I'm full up.

EVERYDAY LIFE

Äha!	suitable for all occasions, also to say sorry
Ja mei!	Well, it's like that! suitable for all occasions, also to say sorry
Gäh weida!	You don't say!
Do legst di nieder!	Hard to believe!
Griaß God!	Hello!/Good morning/ afternoon!
Griaß eich mitnand!	Hello!/Good morning/ afternoon! (for more than one person)
Pfia God!	Good-bye!
Servus!	Hi!/Cheerio!
An scheena Dog no!	Have a nice day!
I mog di!	I like you!
I mog mei Ruah!/ Mei Ruah wui i ham!	I'd like to be left in peace!
Des daugt ma.	I like it.
Des is mia wurscht!	I don't care!
I bin do ned auf da Brennsuppn dahergschwumma!	I'm not stupid!
Des is ghupft wia gschprunga.	Whatever.
Des kon se seng lossn.	That's impressive.
Do host di aba schwer deischt.	Well, there you are completely wrong!

A–Z INDEX

To help you find recipes with particular ingredients quickly and easily, this index lists the most popular ingredients such as **potatoes** or **beef broth**, in alphabetical order and **in bold**, with the relevant recipes.

A

B

C

D

K

L

M

O

P

Q

R

S

T

V

W

Y

INDEX BY CATEGORY

SALADS, STARTERS & SNACKS

SOUPS, STEWS & BROTH

SIDE DISHES

BAKES, GRATINS & SAVOURY BAKING

VEGETARIAN DISHES

WITH PASTA, POTATOES, VEGETABLES & DUMPLINGS

WITH MEAT, POULTRY SAUSAGES & OFFAL

WITH FISH & SEAFOOD

DESSERTS, CAKES & BISCUITS

Monika Schuster

Monika Schuster has always loved to cook and eat. That's why, after training as a hotel manager, she continued her studies and completed a chef's apprenticeship which has enabled her to become a certified master chef. Her outstanding work received recognition when she was awarded the coveted Bavarian State Prize.

Monika Schuster is just as enthusiastic about writing recipes and cookbooks as she is about cooking. So it's no surprise that she also developed a passion for food photography and food-styling. Her love of detail and flair for presentation are reflected in every dish she presents. Her motto? A food photo must taste good!

And our recipe writer's professional tip for her readers is this: the most important thing to have in a kitchen is a good set of tools, like a sharp knife, and proper pots and saucepans. If you've got these, you'll be guaranteed to serve something delicious.

For more information on Monika Schuster, visit her website www.monika-schuster.de

Photo: Sasa Putzar

Anna Cavelius

Anna Cavelius spent most of her childhood in the beautiful upper Bavaria, where she continues to live to this day, right on Lake Ammersee with her two sons.

Having a Bavarian mother, she is of course an expert in Bavarian customs, character and dialect. As her father came from another part of the country, however, she is just as adept at translating Bavarian life philosophies for standard German speakers and new Bavarians. Her love of the country, and the skill required to convey this, is apparent in all her features in this Bavarian cookbook. The vivid stories also contain lots of insider information which you may not easily discover elsewhere.

Anna's belief is that you should only speak Bavarian if you truly know how to do so. And then to explain to the person at the table next to you the proper way to eat a Weisswurst – namely without the skin!

IMPRINT

THE AUTHORS

Monika Schuster, the recipe writer, is a trained cook and master chef and director of the Dallmayr delicatessen gourmet paradise in Munich. She works as a food stylist and develops recipes for numerous clients. Her previous titles include "Low Temperature – Meat and Fish Cooked Gently" for Gräfe und Unzer, which was awarded the gold medal by the Gastronomic Academy of Germany.

Anna Cavelius is a freelance writer and wrote all the features in this book. She studied philosophy in Munich, then continued with linguistics in Siena and Salamanca. Since 1995, she has written on health, lifestyle and culinary topics, including the features in the GU award-winning book "My Heaven on Earth".

THE PHOTOGRAPHER

Klaus-Maria Einwanger, as the photographs in this book show, creates stylish and emotive food photographs at his **food art factory.** He works mostly in southern Munich and London. He found the atmospheric feature images right outside his front door: on the Brünnstein, in Amerang and in Rosenheim ... He was assisted by **Martin Erd** and **Christian Koch; Monika Schuster** and **Anka Köhler** were the food stylists. Equipment, styling and props demonstrate the creativity of **Alexandra Holzer,** with **Mavie Hasenöhrl** as assistant. The rather special picture editing was executed by **Christian Kempf.**

PICTURE CREDITS

All photographs:
Klaus-Maria Einwanger
Syndication:
www.seasons.agency

Project manager: Sigrid Burghard
Editorial assistant:
Monika Bachmeier
Editing, Design, Typesetting/CT:
Redaktionsbüro Christina Kempe, Munich
English edition: Translation:
Sylvia Goulding, Emily Plank;
Editing/Proofreading:
Julie Brooke, Mike Goulding
Cover and Design:
independent Medien-Design, Horst Moser, Munich
Illustrations:
André Gottschalk, Berlin
Production: Susanne Mühldorfer
Proofreading: Barbara Schmidt-Runkel für bookwise GmbH
Test kitchen: Anka Köhler, Munich
Repro: Longo AG, Bolzano, Italy
Printing and binding:
Firmengruppe APPL, Wemding

Environmental note: This book was printed on PEFC-certified paper from sustainable forestry.

ISBN 978-8338-5931-1
1st edition 2016
ISBN of the German edition
978-8338-5788-1

Ein Unternehmen der
GANSKE VERLAGSGRUPPE

OUR GU-GUARANTEE

Dear Reader,

We are delighted that you have chosen a GU book. With your purchase, you're placing your trust in us that the guides will be of high quality, authoritative and up-to-date, and for this we thank you very much! All the information in this guide has been carefully checked. Should it nonetheless contain an error please return the book to our Reader Service with an appropriate note. We will gladly exchange the GU Guide for another one on the same or a similar subject. As a leading publisher of guidebooks we continuously strive to improve our books. Your opinion is important to us. Please send us your suggestions, criticism or praise for our books. Do you have any questions or do you require further advice on a topic? We look forward to hearing from you! We are at your service!

GRÄFE UND UNZER VERLAG

Reader Service
Postfach 86 03 13
D-81630 Munich
Germany
Email:
leserservice@graefe-und-unzer.de

Your GRÄFE UND UNZER Verlag
The guidebook publisher – since 1722.

KV